ROYAL
COMMISSION
ON THE HISTORICAL
MONUMENTS
OF ENGLAND

Stained Glass in England
c.1180-c.1540

Sarah Crewe

LONDON: HER MAJESTY'S STATIONERY OFFICE

Printed in the United Kingdom for Her Majesty's Stationery Office
Dd 240051, 9/87, C35, 45101

Contents

Foreword

The Royal Commission on the Historical Monuments of England has, since 1981, provided a home for the national photographic archive of medieval stained glass. The archive has been formed out of the Royal Commission's existing collections and photographs assembled by the Corpus Vitrearum Medii Aevi, sponsored by the British Academy. The Academy has contributed to the funding and staffing of the archive from the outset.

The International CVMA was founded in 1952 in the aftermath of the Second World War, with its attendant damage to medieval cities such as Coventry, Rouen and Cologne. Its principle aim is the recording and publication of all surviving European medieval stained glass. The British Committee of the CVMA was established in 1956.

This book has grown out of the work of creating the CVMA archive and the selection of photographs reflects both the strengths and weaknesses of the collection. It includes photographs by some of the most important figures in the field of architectural and stained glass photography, such as Herbert Felton and Sidney Pitcher. The work of the Royal Commission's own photographic section is also amply represented, both in the recording of stained glass *in situ* and as a result of regular visits to a number of conservation studios, notably the York Glaziers Trust and Canterbury Cathedral stained glass studio. The co-operation and goodwill of the conservation world remains an invaluable asset in the recording of medieval stained glass.

All the illustrations in this book may be consulted in the Architectural Records Section at the Royal Commission on the Historical Monuments of England, Fortress House, 23 Savile Row, London W1X 1AB. For ease of access to the original photographs, which are arranged by county, the county location of churches is given in parentheses throughout the text. All but three are the copyright of the Royal Commission. My thanks go to the British Academy for permission to reproduce Colour Plate 6 and to Warwickshire County Museums for Plates 13 and 18.

Finally, I would like to thank my colleagues, Stephen Croad and John Bold, in the Architectural Records Section and Terry Buchanan and Tony Rumsey in the Photographic Section for assistance and advice in the preparation of this book, and Jean Irving who has typed and retyped the text with cheerfulness and patience.

SARAH CREWE

Introduction

Few visitors to English cathedrals such as Canterbury, Wells and York can fail to be impressed by the remarkable display of stained glass in the medieval windows. The glass is a splendid but often bewildering dazzle of colour and much of its original meaning and content remains unclear. Apart from the cathedrals, hundreds of parish churches contain substantial remains of stained glass, one of the foremost medieval crafts.

This book is for both the seasoned church visitor and the enthusiastic newcomer. It sets out to explain the basic techniques and development of medieval stained glass and to describe some of the scenes and subjects most commonly encountered, together with some of the sources from which they were derived. It also aims to equip the reader with the means of recognizing glass from successive periods, and perhaps those alien fragments of glass of the wrong style and date which so often detract from an understanding and appreciation of the glass-painter's original intention.

Stained glass is essentially a Christian art form, its popularity stemming from the widely held belief in the mystical relationship between light, glass and the spirit of God. St Bernard of Clairvaux (1090–1153) wrote, 'As the glorious sun penetrates glass without breaking it . . . so the word of God, the Light of the Father, passes through the body of the Virgin, and then leaves it without undergoing any change.' Thus the glazing of the earliest Christian churches was regarded as far more than mere weather-proofing.

Very little stained glass survives in England that can be dated with any confidence to earlier than the second half of the 12th century, and so this book will concentrate on the period c.1180 to c.1540, when changing artistic circumstance and religious upheaval altered forever the traditional environment of the medieval glass-painter. With the coming of the Reformation in the 16th century, accompanied by the Dissolution of the Monasteries, 1536–40, the religious world in which the medieval glass-painter had worked was disrupted and his most important patron was denied him. Consequently, almost no figurative religious glass was produced after the Dissolution, a situation that persisted into the 18th century.

The principles of the medieval craft were further undermined by the introduction in the early 16th century of enamel stains which enabled large areas of white glass to be coloured, without recourse to the traditional practice of cutting and leading.

A generation before the Reformation, however, native glass-painters were under pressure from foreign competition. By 1500, traditional glass-work appeared old-fashioned compared to the work produced on the Continent.

Henry VII employed foreign artists, notably in the execution of his tomb, made by the Italian, Pietro Torrigiani, and during his reign and that of his son, Henry VIII, foreigners filled the post of King's Glazier.

Even outside royal circles, English artists were losing the choice commissions to foreign artists. All twenty-eight windows at Fairford Parish Church (Glos) were glazed by a workshop led by a master from the ancient Low Countries (modern-day Belgium and Holland), and the chapel of Hengrave Hall (Suffolk) was filled by glass probably made by French glass-painters.

This book deals only with medieval stained glass in England. Both Scotland and Wales suffered losses as a result of border warfare in the Middle Ages, the Reformation and, more seriously, through 17th-century Puritanism. Some medieval glass can still be seen in Wales, mostly late in date, but none survives *in situ* in Scotland. (A few excavated fragments can be seen in Holyrood Palace.) Consequently, the greatest wealth of medieval glass is to be found in England, though it is not evenly distributed throughout the country. Counties such as Gloucestershire and Oxfordshire contain interesting glass of all periods while others, such as Surrey and Durham, contain relatively little.

The examples described and panels illustrated are not intended to represent a comprehensive coverage of medieval stained glass in England. The intention has been to include some that are justifiably renowned, together with others that are little known but deserving of appreciation.

1 The Making of Medieval Windows

Although the medieval windows in English churches are usually said to contain 'stained glass' it would, in fact, be more accurate to describe it as 'painted glass'. The colours of a medieval window run throughout the entire thickness of the glass and were imparted by the addition of metal oxides to the glass mix in its molten state. These glasses are known as pot-metals. The details of features, drapery and decoration were, in fact, all painted on to the surface of the coloured glass and were then fired in a kiln. Medieval window glass was hand blown, usually into discs, a process which gives it its characteristic depth and variety of hue. Only at the close of the medieval period did glaziers discover the enamel stains that could be applied to the surface of white glass in order to colour it.

Knowledge of the medieval glass-painter's craft derives almost entirely from one remarkable book, *De Diversis Artibus* (The Various Arts), written by a monk who adopted the pseudonym Theophilus. Although Theophilus reveals little about himself in his treatise, careful study of its contents and of the surviving manuscript copies offers certain clues as to the identity of the author. Theophilus was probably writing in the first half of the 12th century and was almost certainly a German Benedictine. The wealth of practical advice he offers suggests that he was a practising artist, probably a metalworker, which would explain the disproportionate length of the section devoted to this craft. His advice on the making of a window is equally practical and informative, however.

The glass-painter would begin by producing a small preparatory sketch (called a 'vidimus') that would not only serve to crystallize the artist's own ideas but would also help him explain them to his patron. Once a design had been agreed upon, a full-size drawing, or cartoon, would be prepared. The main work of constructing the individual panels was done on a large trestle table coated with whitewash, the preparation of which is described in detail by Theophilus.

The outline of the design was transferred to the surface of the table with the position of the lead strips (calmes) that would hold the pieces of glass in place and the colours of glass to be used all marked. The English artists employed at St Stephen's Chapel, Westminster in 1352 washed the table with ale to fix the design. The pieces of glass to be painted, selected for their colour and quality, could then be placed on the table and, using the charcoal lines visible from beneath as a guide, those areas to be cut out were marked.

Cutting glass to shape in the Middle Ages was highly skilled and difficult as no diamond or steel-wheel cutters were available. The job was laborious, and

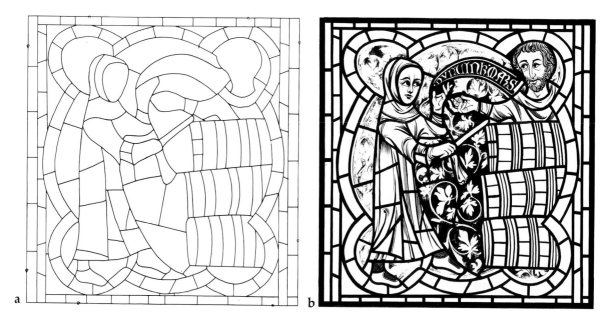

1 *These drawings of a panel of early 14th-century stained glass from the nave clerestory of York Minster have been prepared for the making of a modern replica. Drawing **a** (called the cut-line) shows the outlines of the composition that will be carried by the lead calmes and gives an impression of what the medieval glass-painter would have marked on his whitewashed table. Drawing **b** shows the full cartoon. Not all the later mending leads have been eliminated, in order to convey the present character of the medieval original (Plate 54).*

(Reproduced courtesy of Miss Clare Rawcliffe)

complicated cut-lines are a sure sign of a master glazier at work (Plate 2). The rough shape required was achieved by applying a hot iron to the glass. Theophilus suggested that if the glass did not crack immediately the craftsman should wet the surface with his spittle and try again.

In order to arrive at the exact shape, a grozing iron was used. This was a notched instrument which nibbled away the edges of the glass. Pieces of medieval window glass never have the smooth sharp edge characteristic of glass cut with a modern glass-cutter.

Although the lead lines of a finished window always provided the principal outlines of the design, details of drapery, hair and features were all painted on to the glass (Plate 1) and were then fired in a kiln to ensure permanence. To achieve a variety of lines and modelling effects a wide range of painting techniques were used including the smearing (Plate 3) and dabbing of paint to achieve a stippled effect and the scratching out of a layer of paint to achieve the finest details (Plate 4). The individual pieces would have to be fired several times and at each firing there was always the risk of breakage.

Once all the painting had been successfully completed and the pieces fired, the craftsman returned to his whitewashed table which now provided a work-bench for the assembly of all the parts. The individual pieces were bound together with strips of grooved lead, strong but flexible enough to bend to complex shapes. Nails were tapped into the table to hold the glass and lead

2   *This fine late 12th-century head from Canterbury Cathedral illustrates the high degree of skill necessary to cut the intricately shaped pieces of glass that make up a figure. With the exception of a couple of mending leads in the hair, the lead lines all follow the main outlines of the painting and thus reinforce rather than undermine the design.*

(Canterbury Cathedral, Kent. The choir clerestory. RCHME 1979)

in place while the craftsman worked and the only medieval tables to survive (found at Gerona Cathedral in Spain) bear both the charcoal lines and the nail holes. The completed panel was then bound at its edges with thicker lead and a cement was rubbed in to make the edges of all the joints weather-proof.

Remarkably little is known about the men who made medieval windows. Theophilus implied throughout his account that the designing, painting and execution of a window was in the hands of the same group of craftsmen, but in his craftsman's handbook, Cennino Cennini, a 15th-century Florentine artist, suggested that in Italy it was not unusual for the craftsman to seek the help of a professional draughtsman in the execution of a design.

From the surviving documentary records of glass-painters at work, particularly those dealing with royal commissions, it is clear that they worked in groups or workshops, with craftsmen of varying skills and experience supervised by a master who carried out the most important aspects of the commission himself. All medieval crafts and industries were organized into guilds, associations of craftsmen designed to regulate the craft and its practitioners, to protect standards and prices and to control admission to the craft, or 'Mystery'. Aspiring glass-painters were required to serve a long apprenticeship and were expected to prepare materials and care for tools. Knowledge could only be acquired within this regulated workshop framework which served to protect both craftsman and consumer and only the most experienced and skilled could hope to become master of his own shop.

The responsibility for designing the panels lay with the master, probably in consultation with the patron. Compositions and motifs would be recorded in pattern books for the guidance of the workshop members. Very few artists' sketches or pattern books survive from the medieval period and none can reliably be attributed to a glass-painter's workshop. One exception might be the Guthlac Roll in the British Museum. This vellum roll of *c.*1200 contains eighteen outline drawings within roundels of the Life of St Guthlac of Croyland which may have been a set of designs for a St Guthlac window. It is clear from surviving windows that the same designs were used several times over, with artists sometimes re-using the same full-scale drawings. A single cartoon could be modified slightly or used in reverse to give the impression of variety. In the west window of York Minster, for example, the eight figures of bishops were drawn from only three cartoons.

Whenever a window was commissioned, a contract was drawn up between the workshop and the patron. Lamentably few of these survive and, where they do, the windows to which they refer often do not. Those contracts that can still be studied suggest that the patron of the work specified very clearly what was required of the craftsman. The contract drawn up in 1405 between the Dean and Chapter of York and John Thornton of Coventry, a master glass-painter, stipulated that the east window was to be made in no more than three years and that Thornton himself was to 'paynt the same where need required according to the ordination of the Dean and Chapter' – a clear determination to ensure that the master himself painted the main figures and scenes (Plate 12). Thornton's initials and the date of 1408 appear in the glass as proof that he observed these conditions. In the glazing of the Beauchamp Chapel in St Mary's Church, Warwick, the stipulations of the contract concerned the quality of the materials rather than the craftsmanship. John Prudde was ordered to use only glass of foreign manufacture and thus of the highest quality.

The most valuable commissions emanated from the Court and the most sought-after post was that of King's Glazier. A relative wealth of surviving documentary material, mostly of a financial nature, reveals that the king would call upon the talents of craftsmen from all over England in the decoration of his palaces and buildings. The accounts of 1351–2 for the glazing of St Stephen's Chapel, Westminster, list payments to John de Chestre, William de Walton, John Coventre and John de Lincolne.

John Prudde, one of the few King's Glaziers whose work survives to be admired, was appointed in 1440 (Plate 13). Royal documents record that he was to hold office for life, and in addition to the usual fees, profits and appurtenance was granted a gown of the king's livery every Christmas. Prudde was one of the last Englishmen to hold the post. In 1474 the London glaziers petitioned Edward IV against a number of foreign craftsmen who although not members of the Guild were setting up businesses in London. These foreigners cannot have been without influence however, for Richard III later responded to such protests by banning only the importation of

4 *A detail from the collar of a vestment illustrates how a design could be picked out of a thick layer of paint to reveal the base glass (in this case, white) beneath. The finest details would be scratched out with a needle.*

(York Minster, N Yorks. North choir aisle. RCHME 1969)

completed windows. Thus, by the close of the 15th century, native artists were beginning to lose control of their craft in the face of outside and unregulated competition.

In the reign of Henry VII, the position of native glass-painters was further undermined and it was the Crown that was to emerge as the principal patron of the immigrant Continental artists working in new and strikingly different styles. Henry employed as King's Glazier, Bernard Flower, described in his letters of denization (or naturalization) of 1514 as a native of Almania (or Germany). Another foreigner, Cornelius Meelys, was employed with Flower to repair glass at the Tower of London. Members of the Court followed the royal lead and for the east window of Thornhill Church (W Yorks) Robert Frost, Chancellor to Prince Arthur, employed glaziers working in the new style. Henry VIII continued this trend and in 1517 appointed a Fleming, Galyon Hone, as Flower's successor.

2 An Outline of Window Design

Glass was used by the Romans as a means of weather-proofing window openings although its costliness meant that relatively few buildings had glazed windows. They were, however, regarded from an early date as an important aspect of the decoration of Christian churches. In the 4th century AD, Prudentius wrote of the churches of Constantinople, 'In the round arches of the windows in the basilica shone glass in colours without number,' suggesting that at this date no paint was applied to the glass and confirming the close relationship between coloured glass and mosaic work.

Although window glass had been introduced into Roman Britain, the use of coloured glass in windows can be documented only from Anglo-Saxon times. By the time that Benedict Biscop came to build his monastery churches at Monkwearmouth and Jarrow in the late 7th century, the knowledge of the craft had been lost in Britain and Frankish glaziers had to be employed. Excavations have uncovered fragments of unpainted coloured glass apparently from Biscop's churches. (Colour plate 1). If documentary sources are to be believed, Bishop Wilfred of York had glazed his church against birds and the elements at almost the same date, although no trace of this glazing has ever been found.

Exactly when paint was first applied to coloured window glass is not known. The excavation in 1932 of a painted head in the Carolingian abbey of Lorsch (Hesse, W Germany) shows that painted glass was in use in churches of the 9th century. By the later 11th and early 12th centuries evidence becomes more plentiful, although the earliest painted glass to remain *in situ* in England dates from only the second half of the 12th century. A possible exception may be a panel in All Saints' Church, Dalbury (Derbys), depicting a single and rather rigid figure of St Michael for which a late 11th-century date has been suggested (Plate 5). More extensive series of 12th-century panels can be seen in York Minster and Canterbury Cathedral.

The York panels are survivors from the choir built by Archbishop Roger of Pont L'Eveque and probably date from about 1180. Their varied subject matter (scenes from the Lives of Saints Martin, Nicholas, Benedict, and the Life of Christ) indicate the richness of the Romanesque choir that was torn down in the 14th century. Surviving panels depicting the Last Judgement may have come from the 12th-century west front, also replaced in the 14th century. In an age when what was old was so frequently swept away in favour of what was new and 'modern', their preservation is difficult to understand, but they were re-used in the clerestory of the 14th-century nave, where they were placed against a background of deliberately archaic strapwork.

5   *This figure of St Michael the Archangel is probably one of the earliest examples of* in situ *glazing in England. The paucity of early painted glass makes it difficult to date, but the late 11th century has been suggested. St Michael's hands are raised in the 'orans' position, a motif derived from Byzantine art.*

(All Saints' Church, Dalbury, Derbys. RCHME 1980)

6   *Before reaching the magnificent shrine of St Thomas, the object of their journey, the Canterbury pilgrims encountered a richness and profusion of colour in the single lancet windows of the ambulatory. This photograph, also of this type of window, was taken in 1942 when much of the glass was removed from the Cathedral for safety; the metal armatures that hold the panels of glass in place can clearly be seen.*

(Canterbury Cathedral, Kent. NE Transept. H Felton 1942)

In one church in England it is still possible to experience the atmosphere of a late 12th-century interior. Following a disastrous fire in 1174, the monks of Christchurch Cathedral Priory, Canterbury were forced to rebuild the eastern section of their church. This was achieved in sumptuous style, using the generous offerings of the many pilgrims who came from all over Europe to visit the shrine of the recently cannonized martyr, St Thomas Becket. Glazing was in operation from *c*.1180 to *c*.1220 and despite religious vandalism and the effects of time, much of the glass survives (Plate 2).

The individual narrative panels, contained within geometric shapes, are held in place in the window opening by metal frames or armatures (Plate 6). The figure panels are surrounded by deep borders of rich, fleshy-leaved foliage. The density of patterning and the deep colours, with a predominance of red and blue, combine to create a rich and glowing effect (Colour plate 12). The overall atmosphere of the church must have been mysterious and rather dark, complementing the play of candle-light on the magnificent jewelled shrine of St Thomas Becket which, until its destruction in 1538, was the centre-piece of the choir.

This sort of well-ordered geometric layout persisted into the 13th century, as can be seen in Lincoln Cathedral (Colour plate 11). The great variety of shape found in the Canterbury armatures, appears to have diminished, however, and at Lincoln the circular panel predominates. Only the north rose window approaches Canterbury in the complexity of its patterning.

The poor survival of 12th- and 13th-century glass in English parish churches makes it difficult to judge whether the splendours of York, Canterbury and Lincoln were typical of all windows of the period. It is likely that less wealthy churches were glazed with grisaille (Plate 7), white glass decorated with a foliage design and so called because of its greyish appearance, possibly enlivened with coloured bosses, as in the Lady Chapel of Exeter Cathedral (Devon). However, it was not merely economic considerations that dictated the use of grisaille. By the mid 13th century, architectural taste demanded increasingly lighter church interiors and grisaille was extensively used, even in large churches, cathedrals and secular palaces. The side windows of the chancel at Norbury Church (Derbys) for example, are filled with a remarkable display of early 14th-century grisaille, enlivened with heraldry. The most spectacular surviving example of its extensive use is in the huge Five Sisters Window in the north transept of York Minster (Plate 8), although until the late 18th-century 'restorations' by James Wyatt, Salisbury Cathedral (Wilts) retained much of its original grisaille glazing. In the windows of highest quality, the glass was cut and leaded into intricate and concentric patterns to enhance the painted foliage decoration.

In the last quarter of the 13th century there were subtle changes in the design and layout of windows. The most important of all arose out of evolving architectural fashions. The single lancet openings found at Canterbury (Plate 6), gave way in the second half of the 13th century to large, traceried windows divided by stone mullions, first used extensively in Westminster Abbey and derived ultimately from French sources. English architects adopted these new forms with enthusiasm and the 14th century witnessed an unprecedented richness of architectural decoration triggered off by experimentation with tracery patterns. These new window types, combined with the desire to include greater quantities of light-coloured glass to provide better illumination, led to the evolution of 'band windows' in which rectangular narrative

7   *(right) In 1134, the austere Cistercian Order was forbidden to use figurative glass in the windows of its churches because St Bernard, its founder, believed that it distracted the monks from their religious duties. In humble parish churches, however, grisaille was no doubt commonly used out of financial necessity, using a predominance of the white glass made in England itself and very little of the coloured that had to be imported from the Continent. This example has been restored, but still conveys the original impression.*

(Church of St Mary, Stodmarsh, Kent. F.J. Palmer 1952)

8   *(opposite) The Five Sisters Window of c.1250 is one of the largest surviving expanses of grisaille in Europe. Although the glass has suffered much disturbance and damage, this fine drawing by John Browne, published in 1847, reveals the exceptional quality of the glass, cut and leaded into the most intricate patterns. The painted foliage, set on a delicately cross-hatched background, is of a conventionalized form and creates a light and silvery effect in the north transept.*

(York Minster, N Yorks. Five Sisters Window. RCHME 1977)

Drawn by John Browne.

Etched by J. Browne & Son.

A COMPARTMENT OF ONE OF THE FIVE LIGHTS, IN THE NORTH TRANSEPT.

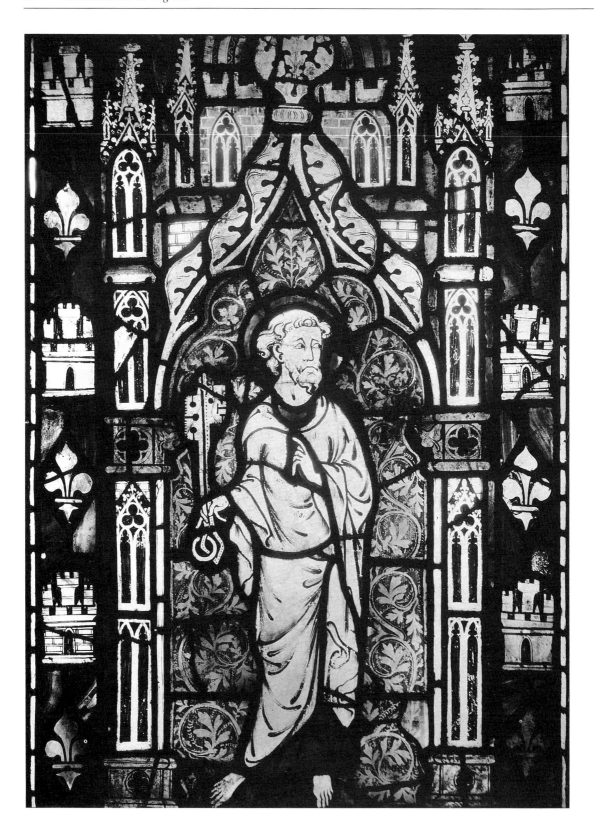

9 *Henry de Mamesfield, Chancellor of Oxford University 1309–12, donated the side windows of Merton College Chapel in the closing years of the 13th century. They already display the principal features of two centuries of window design. The basic canopy has been augmented by brick walls, pinnacles and window traceries. The figure of St Peter stands against a background of naturalized foliage and the narrow borders contain heraldic devices.*

(Merton College Chapel, Oxford, Oxon. RCHME 1938)

panels were arranged in alternating horizontal layers of coloured glass and grisaille or lighter glass (Colour plate 2). The story would usually be read from left to right, starting at the bottom. The lush foliage that formerly spread throughout the window was now confined to narrow borders, and heraldic devices and grotesques were added to the repertoire of motifs.

From the middle of the 13th century, a more naturalistic approach to the depiction of foliage was adopted in both painting and sculpture and is found in glass of the 1280s and 1290s, replacing the conventional forms favoured hitherto. The grisaille in the Chapter House of York Minster (*c.*1285) retains the concentric patterning found in the Five Sisters Window, but is painted with a naturalistic climbing plant, apparently winding through a trellis. In the parish church of Chartham (Kent) this transition to naturalism can be seen in a fascinating series of windows in which the foliage becomes increasingly natural as the glazing proceeds west.

From the late 13th century, figures and scenes which previously had been displayed within geometric shapes were now placed under architectural canopies in imitation of the surrounding architecture. One of the earliest uses of this sort of window, displaying a series of apostles (Plate 9), saints and the repeated kneeling figure of the donor, Henry de Mamesfield, can be seen still in Merton College Chapel, Oxford (*c.*1290).

The earliest canopies were always simple, as in the east window of Selling Church (Kent). By the mid 14th century, however, a growing interest in the depiction of pictorial space led to the elaboration of canopies which were embellished with numerous pinnacles, tiled roofs and traceried windows. They were often enlivened by birds, foliage and even by tiny figures.

The 14th century was also the period in which heraldry became a major element in the decoration of windows. The Peter de Dene Window in York Minster contains so many shields of arms that it is often called the Heraldic Window. Mid 14th-century windows at Tewkesbury, Bristol (Plate 10) and Gloucester all contain heraldic displays.

The choice of coloured glasses used by glass-painters of the 14th century also underwent a transformation. The reds, blues and purples which had predominated previously were replaced by earthy tones of red-brown, yellow and leafy green (Colour plate 3). The most significant new colour emerged in the first decade of the century. By applying and firing a silver compound, usually to the exterior surface of white glass, a yellow stain could be achieved, varying in colour from a delicate silvery tone to a deep orange (Colour plate 4). Throughout the Middle Ages, this was the only colour that could be applied with the brush.

Yellow stain offered enormous advantages, for it could be used to colour small areas that would otherwise require intricate cutting and leading. Thus, a head painted on a single piece of white glass could easily be given golden hair, or a robe a delicately patterned gold border. Although it is most commonly found on white glass, yellow stain could also be used with blue or on the abraded areas of flashed ruby and was thus valuable in illustrating heraldic charges.

In the mid 1300s, the east window of the Abbey Church of Gloucester (now the Cathedral) was filled with some remarkable glass that was to anticipate in some respects the style of the 15th century. The window tracery, in itself innovative, is arranged in a triptych-like fashion and contains a series of saints, kings, nobles, abbots, bishops and apostles, attendant upon the

10   *In 1247 Henry III
ordered that the royal arms,
together with those of his
late father-in-law, the
Count of Provence, be
inserted into the windows of
the hall of Rochester Castle.
This is the first documented
example of the use of
heraldry in English stained
glass. From this date,
heraldry became an
increasingly important
element in the decoration of
windows. This splendid mid
14th-century shield of the
de la Ryvere family adorns
the tracery of Bristol
Cathedral's Lady Chapel
east window.*

*(Bristol Cathedral, Avon. Lady
Chapel. V. Turl c.1940)*

Coronation of the Virgin at the apex. Each figure stands under a vaulted canopy and the pinnacle of each provides the base for the feet of the figure above. The artist displayed a noticeable interest in perspective effects and attempted to create the impression that his figures were standing in sculptured niches.

The most remarkable and significant characteristic of the Gloucester window, however, is its limited palette. The slender and heavily modelled figures, of an almost cadaverous appearance, are painted on white glass (Plate 3), relieved only by the yellow stain and the alternating red and blue of the backgrounds. On a sunny day, the overall effect is a dazzling display of silver, red and blue entirely contradictory to the earthier colour values of earlier 14th-century glass.

The Gloucester experiment was to have few immediate imitators, however. Very little glass survives from the second half of the 14th century; a reflection, perhaps, of the calamitous effects of the plague of the mid century which was responsible for the deaths of numerous artists and patrons alike. Important commissions do survive, however, in Oxford (New College Chapel) and Winchester (the College Chapel), both associated with the workshop of

11 *The west window of Canterbury Cathedral would appear on heraldic evidence to have been commissioned between 1396 and 1399. It shares many of the characteristics of the 'International Gothic' style elsewhere, being finely modelled, with figures of a thick-set, almost stocky, appearance.*

(Canterbury Cathedral, Kent. West window. RCHME 1979)

Thomas of Oxford and the patronage of William of Wykeham, Chancellor of England (1367–71) and Bishop of Winchester (1366–1404).

The New College and Winchester windows, using a large quantity of white glass, are characterized by a softer and more realistic drawing style. This 'soft style' was by no means confined to the circle of glaziers employed by Wykeham. In York, John Burgh was employed from 1399 to 1419 as principal glazier to the Minster and his windows in the Lady Chapel share many of the same characteristics. A particularly fine and until recently unappreciated example of late 14th-century glass-painting survives in the west window of Canterbury Cathedral. This magnificent window contains a splendid series of figures of kings (Plate 11) and may have been a commemoration of the ill-fated Richard II.

The soft style reached its apogee in the first half of the 15th century. One of its most talented exponents came from the Midlands city of Coventry. John Thornton arrived in York from Coventry in 1405 to glaze the Minster east window and his workshop was to dominate York glass-painting for fifty years. Although a fine series of angels in a style not unlike Thornton's survives from the bombed Cathedral of Coventry (formerly the parish church of St Michael), little is known of Thornton's early career and training.

The work of Thornton and his contemporaries is often highly realistic and finely modelled (Plate 12). In the best work of the period, figures are strongly characterized, and it is easy to believe that the artists had studied their fellow citizens for inspiration. It seems likely, however, that Thornton and his workshop were also conscious of contemporary developments in painting and sculpture on the Continent, where craftsmen shared many of the same artistic interests. The proximity of the port of Hull meant that work by artists in Germany and the Low Countries was easily accessible to those in York. Nowhere is this feeling stronger than in Thornton's masterpiece, the great east window of York Minster.

Another characteristic of 15th-century glass is its colour range (Colour plate 5). The colour combinations of Gloucester were now taken up in earnest and

12 *John Thornton's great masterpiece, the east window of York Minster, is characterized by the imaginative way he handles the difficult text of the Book of Revelation and the startling reality of his figures. Male heads are particularly finely drawn, often with rather large and bulbous noses, highlighted at the tip. From the size of the window and the short time in which the commission was completed, it may be assumed that Thornton headed a large workshop.*

(York Minster, N Yorks. East window. RCHME 1970)

13 *John Prudde's splendid figures of St Thomas Becket and St Alban reflect not only the wealth of Richard Beauchamp, Earl of Warwick, but also the increasingly sumptuous tastes of Court circles. Note the 'jewels' leaded into the hems of the robes and the mitre of the Archbishop.*

(Beauchamp Chapel, St Mary's Church, Warwick, Warwicks. P.B. Chatwin c.1966)

white glass and yellow stain dominate, the commonest pot-metal colours being blue and red. Spatial experiments were also pursued and canopies became yet more elaborate creations, frequently inhabited by small figures set in niches (Plate 24). Inscriptions were now painted in the black letter script that in the course of the 14th century had superseded the Lombardic capitals of the 12th and 13th centuries.

Glass of the 15th century survives in churches throughout England. Particularly fine sets of windows can be seen in Great Malvern Priory Church (Hereford & Worcester) and All Souls College Chapel, Oxford (Plate 29). The rich remnants found in Norfolk attest to the wealth of the county in this period and to the importance of Norwich as a glass-painting centre.

From the middle of the 15th century onwards there was a gradual return to the use of richer colours. For example, the glass from the east window of Holy Trinity, Tattershall (Lincs), which is now divided between St Martin's Church, Stamford (Lincs) and nearby Burghley House (Cambs), includes a rich purple and deep green in its colour scheme, together with a jewelled effect for hems and hangings. In some cases the glass would actually be drilled to admit different coloured 'jewels'. In other instances, attempts were made to fuse coloured fragments on to the white glass, although these experiments were often not successful.

One of the most spectacular displays of jewelled glass can be seen in John Prudde's work in the Beauchamp Chapel of St Mary's, Warwick (Plate 13). Glass-painters of the period also displayed a pronounced interest in details of contemporary dress, often of a rather exotic nature. The figure of the Emperor Nero in the east window of St Peter Mancroft, Norwich (Norfolk), for example, wears a richly furred short gown and heavy, low-slung belt (Plate 53).

It was also in this period, however, that some English glass-painting styles began to look old-fashioned when compared with the best work on the Continent. The bold, strongly linear painting style used to great effect in the St Peter Mancroft glass tended to look harsh and rather crude in poorer quality work.

The way in which foreign, and in particular Flemish, glass-painters were encouraged to settle in England has already been described. Suffice to say that from the close of the 15th century to the Reformation the best commissions were lost by craftsmen working in traditional styles and went either to foreigners working in England or to those native artists who were able to adapt themselves to new fashions.

Painted glass of the early 16th century is in marked contrast to the work of the previous century. The traditional canopied frame is largely abandoned in favour of a more realistic spatial setting. The narrative often spreads across the lights, disregarding the structural divisions of windows still Gothic in design. In the great windows of King's College Chapel, Cambridge, the scenes unfold across the whole window and have a clearly delineated foreground, middle ground and background. Landscapes are well developed and the complex architectural features are decorated with Renaissance motifs, at odds with the architecture of the Chapel itself, which is one of the masterpieces of fan-vaulted English Gothic.

The figure style of this period was in imitation of easel painting, being highly modelled with heavy stippling. Figures were often of a rather solid and bulky nature, depicted with great vigour. Figure style and particularly the drawing of highly individualized faces full of character (Colour plate 6) reveals

14　*A detail from the Fairford Crucifixion revealing the skill of early 16th-century glass painters in manipulating their characters in space. The scene, crammed with mounted figures, unfolds across several lights and, as in the Cambridge windows, little account is taken of the limitations of the architectural setting. In the case of Christ and the crucified thief, legibility has been marred by paint loss.*

(Church of St Mary, Fairford, Glos. RCHME 1972)

the influence of artists from the Low Countries. For about a hundred years, these artists had been developing a style that strove to reflect the vigorous and bustling life of their mercantile, urban society. The dainty, mannered styles favoured by courtly patrons were eschewed by both painters and sculptors alike, whose robust and strikingly life-like figures expressed the values and ideals of a new class of patron, whose wealth came not from land but from trade.

The overall impression given by a 16th-century window can be confusing. Narrative scenes are crowded (Plate 14), reflecting the multiplicity of visual sources drawn upon, and intelligibility was not enhanced by ambitious spatial settings. The problem has often been further exacerbated by paint loss from much 16th-century glass. This may be the result of under-firing of the paint in an attempt to preserve as much of the tonal wash and stipple shading as possible, as it would be these lighter effects which would normally be most vulnerable in the firing process. Close examination soon reveals, however, the great virtuosity and technical skill of these glass-painters.

Many writers have viewed these new styles, so strongly influenced by Renaissance ideas, as the beginning of a long decline in the glass-painter's art, representing as they did a denial of the essentially two-dimensional nature of the medium. It was also at this date that enamels began to appear in English painted glass, and these probably presented a more serious challenge to the traditional principles of cutting and leading, although initially they were used mainly in heraldic glass.

At this crucial time the art of glass-painting was denied any further natural evolution by the upheavals of the Reformation, with its injunctions against superstitious imagery, and the effects of Monastic Dissolution. The Church had always been the greatest patron of the glass-painter and, although demand for secular subjects and heraldry continued after the Reformation, secular patrons alone could not fill the void left by the Church.

In the middle of the 16th century the art of glass-painting in England entered a dark period. Only in the 19th century did the traditional art experience a true revival, through a careful study of the techniques and styles of the medieval masters.

3 The Role of the Donor

The donor, or patron, whose portrait sometimes survives in the window for which he paid, remains a shadowy figure. In many instances, he or she is anonymous and only the type of window or mode of dress reveals something of background and social status. The portrait was rarely drawn from life and it is possible in relatively few cases to learn anything of the donor's personal history or the circumstances in which his gift was made. The identification of a donor can, however, be of great use in dating a window. In the Magnificat Window at Great Malvern Priory, for example, the inscriptions ask for the prayers of the onlooker for the good health of Prince Arthur and his wife Katherine of Aragon. Their wedding had taken place on 14 November 1501 and the Prince died on 2 April 1502, allowing the window to be dated quite precisely.

Despite the anonymity of so many donors it is nevertheless possible to appreciate the variety of men and women involved in the patronage of the medieval glazier's art. The importance of the donor's role must never be underestimated for, throughout the Middle Ages, the artist worked to strict instructions laid down by his patron, in circumstances that would be intolerable to many modern artists. The amount of money that a donor was able to spend determined, as it would today, the complexity of the commission. At Waterperry in Oxfordshire, for example, a relatively humble couple, presumably man and wife, paid for a simple window with figures set directly into small diamond-shaped panes, or quarries, of a repeated design which was easy and cheap to produce. In another window in the same church are kneeling figures of Robert FitzEllis, the tenant of the manor and Margaret, his wife. This glass, dating from the 1460s, is of high quality, displaying fine detail and skilful back-painting (Plate 15), thus reflecting the greater wealth and status of the donor.

The high cost of glazing presumably accounts for the fascinating windows in the church of St Neot's, Cornwall where, according to inscriptions, windows were paid for by groups of young men and women and the wives of the parish. Another example of group patronage survives in Ludlow Church (Shrops), where the Palmers' Guild (a guild of pilgrims established in the 14th century and dedicated to St John the Evangelist) paid for a window depicting the story of St Edward the Confessor and the Pilgrim.

Some of the most splendid commissions came from royal or noble patrons. Although the exact nature of Edward IV's involvement in the glazing of the Royal Window at Canterbury is not known, the King is represented kneeling at a beautifully detailed prie-dieu (Plate 16) accompanied by his wife,

15   *This portrait of Margaret FitzEllis and a small girl (either her daughter Margery, or niece Sybil) was painted in the 1460s. That it was an expensive commission is indicated by the superb detailing of their dress, with necklaces and finger rings picked out in yellow stain, and by the extreme delicacy of the painting. The shadowy quality of the hair-net under Margaret's veil has been achieved by painting on the reverse of the glass.*

(Church of St Mary, Waterperry, Oxon. RCHME 1972)

16   *The Royal Window, planned sometime after May 1482, shows Edward IV, his wife and surviving children, including the ill-fated 'Princes in the Tower'. Here we see Edward himself kneeling at a prie-dieu decorated with an image of St George. The rose of York decorates the hangings behind him, and the inscription recalls his claim to be King of England and France and Lord of Scotland.*

(Canterbury Cathedral, Kent. North-west transept. RCHME 1973)

17   *This window, restored in 1873, is said to have come from Stretton Sugwas, where the medieval bishops of Hereford had a residence. It contains saints of local relevance (St Ethelbert and St Thomas Cantelupe) and was the gift of a bishop, who is seen here kneeling at the feet of St Anne and the Virgin Mary. Although he has no identifying label, he may be Bishop Thomas Spofford (1421–43) whose initials appear in fragments elsewhere in the church.*

(Church of St Mary, Ross-on-Wye, Hereford & Worcester. S. Pitcher c.1924)

Elizabeth Woodville, and their surviving sons and daughters. The Princess Elizabeth later appears as Queen in a window donated by her husband, Henry VII in the north transept of Great Malvern Priory. The west window of the same church had been the gift of Richard, Duke of Gloucester, afterwards Richard III.

Richard, Earl of Warwick, died in 1439 and in his will made provision for the building of a chapel in St Mary's Church, Warwick that was to be the equal of anything built by kings. Between 1443 and its consecration in 1475 the enormous sum of £2,481 4s 7d was spent and John Prudde, the King's Glazier, was employed to fill the east window with painted glass (Plates 13 and 18).

Princes of the Church were also important donors (Plate 17). York Minster had particularly generous patrons amongst its higher clergy. Windows in the nave were donated by Archbishop Greenfield and Chancellor Ripplingham and in 1339 Archbishop Melton gave the west window of the nave (Colour plate 2). In the 15th century, windows in the north aisle of the choir were donated by Henry Bowet, Archbishop from 1407 to 1423, Thomas Parker, Prebendary of Ampleforth from 1410 to 1423, and Robert Wolveden, Treasurer of York from 1426 to 1432. Probably the most impressive of episcopal glazing commissions came from William of Wykeham, who as Bishop of Winchester (1366–1404) had enormous funds at his disposal. With them he founded

18 *(left) The donor portrait of Richard Beauchamp, Earl of Warwick, exists only in a damaged state in the glass of the Beauchamp Chapel. The identity of the donor is made abundantly clear, however, by the presence of the muzzled bear of Warwick throughout the borders and backgrounds of the glass.*
This detail also shows the prophet figure embroidered on the apparel of St Thomas Becket's vestment (see Plate 13).

(Beauchamp Chapel, St Mary's Church, Warwick, Warwicks. P.B. Chatwin c.1966)

19 *(right) The 14th-century glass of the east window of St Peter's Church, Aldwincle commemorates two of its rectors. This panel depicts Roger Estravers.*

(Church of St Peter, Aldwincle, Northants. RCHME 1985)

Winchester College and New College, Oxford and filled the chapels of both with sumptuous glass.

More lowly clergy were often involved in the beautification of the parish church (Plate 19). In 15th-century York, Robert Semer, Vicar of St Martin-le-Grand donated the west window (Plate 41) of his church and John Walker, Rector of Holy Trinity Goodramgate, York, gave the east window of his (Plate 22). In the Church of St Leonard, Waterstock (Oxon), John Brown, Rector from 1469 to 1500 commemorated both himself and his father, Thomas.

Although the exact role of a donor in the choice of scene and subject remains unclear, it seems likely that it was the donor, perhaps if he were a layman with the guidance of his parish priest, who made these choices. In the many references to glazing programmes in Henry III's palaces, it is clear that the King himself specified quite clearly what the subjects were to be. The story of Dives and Lazarus was a particular favourite. Even when no contract survives, the wishes of the donor can often clearly be discerned. The famous Bell-founder's Window in the nave of York Minster displays scenes from the profession of its donor, Richard Tunnoc, bell-founder, alongside scenes from the life of St William of York. Yet another York window, given by a citizen called Vincent, depicts in one of its main lights the Martyrdom of St Vincent, the donor's name saint. This was probably one of the commonest ways in

20 *(left) The east window of St Peter and St Paul, East Harling originally contained the kneeling figures of Anne Harling and two of her husbands, Sir William Chamberlain (died 1462) and Sir Robert Wingfield (died 1480), pictured here wearing a heraldic surcoat. The window was presumably glazed at the expense of Anne, a considerable heiress, who outlived Sir William and Sir Robert, her third husband being John, Lord Scrope of Bolton. When she herself died in 1498, she left money for windows at Wymondham Abbey, the Cambridge White Friars and Castle Acre and West Acre Priories.*

(Church of St Peter and St Paul, East Harling, Norfolk. D. King 1947–8)

21 *(right) William Browne of Stamford was 'a marchant of a very wonderful richenesse' (William Dugdale) and a member of the Calais Wool Staple. At the time of his death in 1489 William had seen only the chapel of his new hospital through to completion. The rest of the foundation was built under the supervision of his brother-in-law, Thomas Stokke. This roundel in the audit room shows William's stork device and motto: [God] me spede.*

(Browne's Hospital, Stamford, Lincs. RCHME 1973)

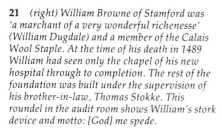

which a donor expressed himself in the choice of subject matter for his window (Colour plate 7).

Another popular way for donors to be represented was by heraldic display. Donor figures are often identifiable by heraldic devices on their clothing (Plate 20), but in some cases an array of family heraldry took the place of a figure. The parish church of Moccas (Hereford & Worcester) stands only a few hundred yards from the manor house. In the 14th century the church was glazed at the behest of the Lord of the Manor, de Frenes, who not surprisingly saw to it that the de Frenes arms were glazed into all the tracery lights and were incorporated into the architectural canopies in the main lights.

Personal badges and mottoes could also be used as a reference to the donor. William Browne, a Stamford merchant, founded a hospital for the care of poor men and women. The building was not completed until 1494 and Browne's personal badge and motto appear several times in the glass (Plate 21), together with his arms and his merchant's mark. The recipients of his charity would be in no doubt as to the identity of their benefactor.

The rebus, a visual pun upon parts of a name, which is common in carved form, also appears in glass. Two windows in All Saints' Church, Weston-on-Avon (Warwicks) contain quarries depicting a cook's table resting on a ship on the sea, a rather laborious reference to the Cooksey family. A simpler example survives in the Canterbury north-west transept where James Goldwell, Bishop of Norwich (1472–99) is represented by a shield bearing a gold well, while at Shelton (Norfolk), a cockle-shell on a barrel (or tun) recalls the Shelton donors.

4 Subjects and Sources

Medieval Europe was a world with a universal language, Latin, in which the Church's liturgy and much secular knowledge was transmitted. The medieval bible was the Vulgate, translated from Hebrew and Greek into Latin by St Jerome in c.400. Throughout the Middle Ages the majority of men and women were, however, illiterate. Learning and the possession of books was restricted to a small number of churchmen, monks and those laymen for whom it was either a prerequisite of high social status or an accomplishment necessary to the successful pursuit of a profession or of commerce. For the unlettered, therefore, religious knowledge was acquired not from reading the Bible but by instruction from the pulpit and from the religious drama enacted on various feast days, reinforced by the decorative cycles adorning the windows and walls of the churches. Scenes were often accompanied by scrolls bearing inscriptions, but it must be assumed that, for the majority, the emblems and attributes held by the saints were the principal means of identification.

The subject matter surviving in English stained glass is now but a fraction of what could have been found on the eve of the Reformation. Quite apart from the losses sustained through the dissolution and demolition of many monastic churches, certain Protestant clergy were zealous in their attacks on what they considered to be superstitious images. Dean Horne of Durham (1551–53), for example, 'pulled downe and broke all to pieces' the St Cuthbert Windows in the Cathedral cloister. Thomas Becket, opponent of Henry II, martyred in 1170 and canonized in 1173, aroused the particular animosity of Henry VIII. By his order, Becket's shrine at Canterbury was dismantled and all images of him and references to him in the liturgy were expunged.

Further damage was wreaked by the Puritans of the 17th century. Ordinances issued in 1643 and 1644 were directed against images of the Virgin Mary, Christ on the Cross and the Three Persons of the Trinity in particular (Plate 22). Parliamentary 'visitors' were appointed, and William Dowsing, who 'visited' Norfolk and Cambridgeshire, was responsible for the destruction of over seven thousand images. Renewed attacks on the Canterbury glass can be seen in an oil painting by Thomas Johnson (dated 1657 but probably depicting events of the 1640s), where the iconoclasts are shown at work on the windows in the south aisle.

From surviving windows it is, none the less, possible to reconstruct an impression of the relative popularity of different subjects in successive periods. In churches of the 12th and 13th centuries, typological windows, in which events in the Old Testament were shown to be prefigurations of events in the Life of Christ, appear to have been favoured. The three days spent by

22 *This fascinating panel in the east window of Holy Trinity, Goodramgate, York, shows the Coronation of the Virgin at the hands of the Trinity, represented quite literally as three persons. As this sort of subject was considered superstitious, not to mention blasphemous, by the Reformed Church, representations of it are now rare.*

(Church of Holy Trinity, Goodramgate, York, N Yorks. RCHME 1974)

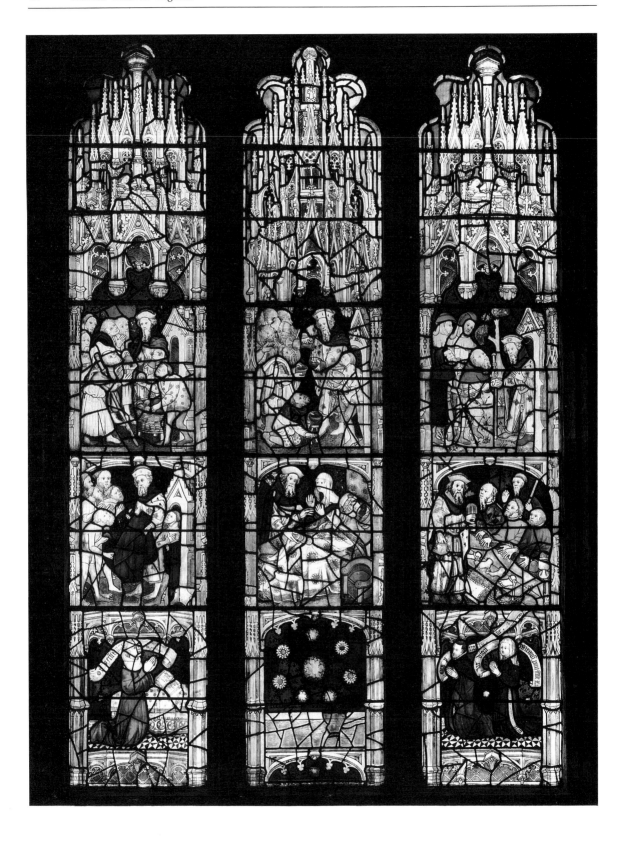

23 *This window in a York parish church is devoted to the narration of six of the Seven Corporal Acts of Mercy. A wealthy citizen is shown clothing the naked, visiting the sick, relieving those in prison, feeding the hungry, giving drink to the thirsty and welcoming the stranger, in accordance with Christ's commandments. The donors and canopies are original to the church, but do not belong to this window.*

(All Saints' Church, North Street, York, N Yorks. RCHME 1957)

Jonah in the belly of the whale were thus seen as a precursor of the period between Christ's death and resurrection. Windows with this rather academic approach to biblical narrative filled the monks' choir at Canterbury, in marked contrast to the more lively Becket miracle scenes in the ambulatory, designed to be seen by visiting pilgrims. At least seven Old Testament scenes from the 13th-century windows at Lincoln could be from typological windows and a panel depicting Daniel in the lion's den suggests that similar windows once adorned the Romanesque choir of York Minster.

The Lives of the Saints were popular subjects for windows throughout the Middle Ages. In the 14th century, however, single figures or individual incidents, often martyrdoms or tortures, identified by the appropriate emblem, were particularly popular. Large narrative cycles in glass are rare survivals from this period, although the remains of a series illustrating episodes from Genesis and the Infancy and Passion of Christ survive in St Mary's Church, Newark (Notts).

The narrative window enjoyed renewed popularity in the 15th and early 16th centuries (Plate 23), encouraged perhaps by the success of the mystery plays which, from the late 14th-century, were performed in English rather than in Latin. Interest in Old Testament and typological subjects also revived and important remains survive at Great Malvern Priory, where there were once windows devoted to Noah, Abraham, Jacob, Joseph, Moses and Aaron, and at Thaxted (Essex), where four much-damaged panels depict episodes from Genesis. The contract for the windows at King's College Chapel, Cambridge, stipulated that they should reveal the 'Olde Law and the Newe', derived largely from the *Biblia Pauperum* (the Bible of the Poor) and *Speculum Humanae Salvationis* (the Mirror of Man's Salvation), the typological pictorial bibles that were the commonest sources for biblical compositions throughout the Middle Ages.

The most popular source of information on the Lives of the Saints was the *Golden Legend*, compiled in the mid 13th century by the Dominican, Jacobus de Voragine, and translated into French by Jean de Vigny in the 14th century. Caxton produced an English edition in 1483. These legends were plundered for easily recognizable emblems to serve as a means of identification, usually taken from the events surrounding a saint's death. Thus St Clement is shown with the anchor to which he was tied and thrown into the sea (Plate 25), St Lawrence carries the grid-iron on which he was burnt (Colour plate 5), St Blaise carries the wool comb with which the flesh was torn from his body (e.g. in St John's Church, Stamford), and St Bartholomew carries the knife with which he was flayed. In more grisly examples, he even carries his own flayed skin over his arm, as at Acaster Malbis (N Yorks) and Grappenhall (Cheshire).

Other commonly portrayed male saints include Peter (the keys to the Kingdom of Heaven), Paul (the sword of martyrdom), John the Baptist (clad in the camel skin he wore in the wilderness, sometimes with the hooves still attached) (Plate 24) and John the Evangelist (holding a chalice from which flees poison in the form of a dragon) (Plate 26). Another very popular saint was Nicholas of Myra, whose character gave rise to Santa Claus and to whom whole windows were dedicated at North Moreton (Berks) and Hillesden (Bucks). St Christopher was as common in glass as in wall paintings. In a remarkable although fragmented panel at Birtsmorton (Hereford & Worcester) the rarely portrayed scene of his baptism by the Christ child survives.

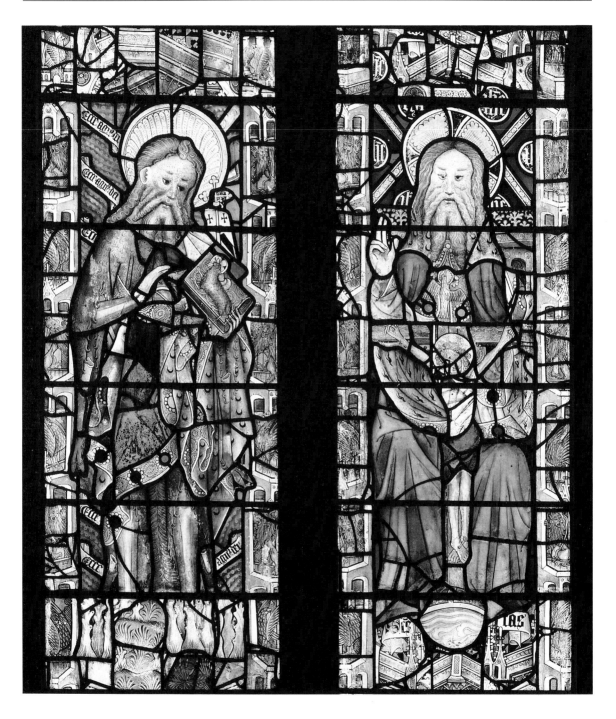

24   *St John the Baptist appears in typical medieval guise, holding the* **Agnus Dei** *(lamb of God) and dressed in a camel skin, with legs and hooves (with bare bones protruding) still attached. In the adjoining light, is a representation of the Trinity, this time of the 'Mercy Seat' type, with God the Father supporting the crucified Christ accompanied by the Holy Spirit in the form of a dove.*

(Chapel of Browne's Hospital, Stamford, Lincs. RCHME 1973).

26   *St John the Evangelist was commonly represented, as here, holding a chalice from which a dragon or viper escapes. This refers to the legendary challenge from the high priest of Diana at Ephesus to drink from a poisoned cup. Upon blessing the cup, St John drank, and of course survived.*

(Church of St Mary, Orchardleigh, Somerset. S. Pitcher c.1946)

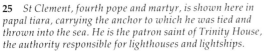

25   *St Clement, fourth pope and martyr, is shown here in papal tiara, carrying the anchor to which he was tied and thrown into the sea. He is the patron saint of Trinity House, the authority responsible for lighthouses and lightships.*

(Church of St Peter, Stockerston, Leics. RCHME 1983)

Several English royal saints can also be found in glass. One of the windows at Ludlow is devoted to the Legend of St Edward the Confessor and St John the Evangelist who, disguised as a pilgrim, was given a ring by St Edward as an act of charity. This legend is also commemorated in the choir aisle of York Minster. The Anglo-Saxon martyr, King Edmund of East Anglia, appears at Upper Hardres (Kent) and Saxlingham Nethergate (Norfolk). A crowned female figure holding a cross staff in St Mary Magdalene's Church, North Ockendon (now in Gtr London, but formerly Essex), may represent St Ethelburga, Abbess of Barking in Essex who was reputed to be of royal blood.

Female saints were also often depicted with reminders of their sufferings for the faith. St Catherine, with the spiked wheel on which she was tortured (Plate 29) and St Margaret, with the dragon that devoured her (Plate 55), were two of the most popular, although it is probable that neither ever existed. They appear in the same window at Diddington (Cambs). Apollonia always holds the pincers with which her teeth were drawn (e.g. Charlynch in Somerset), while St Barbara carries the tower in which she was immured (e.g. Loders in Dorset). Rather less bloodthirsty items identify St Mary Magdalene, who carries the pot of ointment that she took to Christ's empty tomb, as at Bredon (Hereford & Worcester), where she is paired with St Mary of Egypt, and St Dorothy who carries the flowers that grew up at the place of her martyrdom.

A saint whose popularity in England is no longer matched by surviving representations in glass was St Helen, discoverer of the true cross and mother of Constantine, the first Christian emperor. A completely spurious story supported by the chronicler Geoffrey of Monmouth (d.1154) claimed that she was of British origin, being the daughter of King Coel (Old King Cole!) of Colchester. One hundred and thirty-five English churches were dedicated to her and at Ashton-under-Lyne (Gtr Manchester) there are eighteen panels depicting her life. Another popular female saint, whose help was sought by housewives and serving maids, was the faithful and pious St Sitha, a 13th-century Italian maidservant who is usually shown carrying the house-hold keys that were miraculously restored to her.

Saints could also be identified by events associated with later developments in their cults. Thus St James the Great is always shown as a pilgrim to his own shrine at Santiago de Compostela, probably the most popular of all pilgrimage destinations in medieval Europe (Plate 27). St Anthony Abbot is usually dressed as a member of the Order that was dedicated to him and is accompanied by a pig wearing a bell, a reference to the special privilege of the Order by which their pigs were allowed to roam freely (e.g. Munslow in Shropshire). St Cuthbert is often represented, as in Oxford Cathedral, carrying the head of the sainted Northumbrian king, Oswald. After the sack of the holy island of Lindisfarne by the Danes in AD 875, the relics of both saints were moved throughout Northumbria together. Both found a permanent home at Durham in AD 995 and were found in the same tomb when it was opened in 1827.

Evidence for localized 'cults' can also be found in stained glass. Thus a whole window at Great Malvern is dedicated to the Saxon, St Werstan, the Priory's founder (Plate 28), and the Life of St Neot unfolds in a window at St Neot in Cornwall. The relatively short-lived popularity of St Thomas Cantelupe of Hereford is commemorated by a figure of the Saint paired with St Thomas Becket at the local church of Credenhill and in St Mary's, Ross-on-Wye (Hereford & Worcester). St Frideswide, founder of the priory church that

27 *St James the Great is shown here in his commonest guise, dressed as a pilgrim. Although Reading Abbey claimed to have one of the saint's hands among its relics, it was to Spain that most pilgrims journeyed, returning with the cockleshell badge of Santiago de Compostela worn here by the saint himself.*

(Church of St Mary, East Brent, Somerset. S. Pitcher c.1946)

28 *In this clerestory window in the priory church of Great Malvern, the Saxon-hermit St Werstan witnesses a vision of angels consecrating the chapel that he was to build.*

(Great Malvern Priory, Hereford & Worcester. North choir clerestory. S Pitcher c.1936)

is now Christ Church Cathedral, Oxford, appears in the Cathedral glass, in Trinity College Library and in the nearby parish church of Kidlington. St Sidwell, beheaded by a scythe and buried outside the City of Exeter, appears in the Cathedral east window. She also appears in All Souls College Chapel, Oxford, where her presence is explained by the Exeter connections of the supervisor of the college buildings, Roger Keyes (Plate 29).

Throughout the Middle Ages, various unofficial saints were revered in England. Cults were associated with Thomas of Lancaster, Edward II and Archbishop Richard Scrope of York, although none were ever formally recognized by the Church. Another such saint was the hermit, Robert of Knaresborough (1160–1218), revered at Dale Abbey, Derbyshire. He appears in the glass from the Abbey that can be seen now in St Matthew's Church, Morley (Derbys).

Despite the ferocity of Puritan attacks on windows devoted to the Lives of the Virgin and of Christ, examples of both types of window survive. The east window of Hengrave Hall (Suffolk), being in a private chapel, was less vulnerable to damage and preserves an Infancy and Passion of Christ series (Colour plate 8). Other examples survive at Great Malvern Priory and East Harling (Norfolk).

The numerous examples of stranded figures of the mourning Virgin and St John, as at Arlingham (Glos), suggest that iconoclasm directed against the figure of Christ on the Cross has taken its toll. None the less, many fine Crucifixion compositions survive, a particularly moving one being in the east window of Eaton Bishop Church (Hereford & Worcs).

Although the majority of scenes involving Christ were derived from biblical sources, some were drawn from apocryphal accounts. In the glass at Fairford Church (Glos), for example, the resurrected Christ is shown appearing to the Virgin, an event that does not figure in the biblical account. In other cases, the artists have drawn upon popular sources or from their own imaginations (Plate 30).

The apocryphal literature surrounding the life of the Virgin Mary reflected the strength of English devotion to her throughout the Middle Ages. Books such as the *Proto-evangelium of James* and the *Gospel of Pseudo-Matthew* provided many colourful details of the parentage and infancy of the Virgin and of her death and Assumption into Heaven, where she was received and crowned by her Son. A whole window at Great Malvern Priory was devoted to her birth, infancy and early life. The story of how St Joseph was chosen as her husband is depicted at Lincoln and she can be seen with her mother, St Anne, in glass (Plate 17) at Ross-on-Wye (Hereford & Worcester). A window in the York Chapter House describes the events surrounding her death. The apostles were miraculously gathered to her death-bed and then carried her bier at her funeral. A disrespectful Jew tried to overturn the bier, but his hands stuck painfully to its underside and he was carried along until St Peter intervened to convert and free him. The Virgin's subsequent Assumption into Heaven survives at East Harling, while at Beckley (Oxon), a rare version can be seen in which the ascending virgin, supported by angels, drops her girdle to St Thomas who had previously refused to believe in this miraculous event (Plate 31). The obvious parallel with Thomas's role in the Life of Christ reveals that the apocryphal authors were anxious that their stories of the Virgin should closely mirror the biblical accounts of Christ's life and death. Her Life culminated in her coronation as Queen of Heaven (Plate 32).

29   *On 13 May 1441 John Glazier of Oxford was paid for eight windows in the Chapel of All Souls College, including the one containing these three graceful female figures. All three are labelled. Etheldreda, an Anglo-Saxon queen and Abbess of Ely, is shown with crozier and crown; Catherine holds the wheel on which she was tortured and the sword of her martyrdom, while Sidwell (labelled Sativola) in a rare appearance in English glass, holds the scythe with which she was beheaded.*

(All Souls College Chapel, Oxford, Oxon. RCHME 1936)

30   *(left) This 15th-century panel, painted with great vigour, depicts Christ being fastened to the cross. The enactment of such scenes in religious plays no doubt affected the way in which such pictures were conceived. Recent restoration replaced the missing left-hand side of Christ's torso.*

(Church of St Peter, Stockerston, Leics. RCHME 1983)

31   *(above) In this tracery light is a rarely represented scene in the Legend of the Virgin. As she is raised up to Heaven by angels she drops her girdle to the apostle Thomas who is seen with hands outstretched to receive it. This second instance of Thomas's incredulity derives from apocryphal rather than Biblical sources.*

(Church of St Mary the Virgin, Beckley, Oxon. RCHME 1972)

32   *An early 14th-century
tracery panel shows the
enthroned and crowned
Virgin receiving the blessing
of Christ.*

*(All Saints' Church, Wing,
Bucks. RCHME 1980)*

A popular medieval subject that honoured both the Virgin and her Son was the Tree of Jesse, which evolved as a pictorial means of portraying prophecy. A tree or vine is shown springing from the recumbent figure of Jesse. Its branches are inhabited by prophets and Christ's royal ancestors, and culminate with the Virgin and Christ. The subject was current throughout the Middle Ages, with 12th-century fragments surviving at both Canterbury and York. The 14th century witnessed an increase in its popularity, with an especially large number surviving in the West Midlands and West Country. Fragmentary trees survive at Merevale and Mancetter (Warwicks) and Madley (Hereford & Worcester), with restored examples at Ludlow, Shrewsbury and Bristol Cathedral. A particularly interesting example fills the north chancel window of Dorchester Abbey (Oxon). In this instance, glass and stone together form the tree. The subject enjoyed renewed popularity in the late 15th and 16th centuries and there are fine examples at Leverington (Cambs) and Margaretting (Essex).

The Last Judgement provided a fruitful area for the exercise of the medieval imagination. The tracery of Carlisle Cathedral's east window contains lively scenes of the general resurrection, with the Blessed moving up to Heaven and the Damned heading for Hell. St Michael usually plays a prominent role in these proceedings, often shown weighing souls in his scales to decide their fate. A particularly impressive version of the Last Judgement survives in the west window of Fairford Church (restored at its upper level), complete with the Torments of Hell, illustrated with great vigour and imagination. Another version, now sadly faded, fills the east window of the Savile Chapel of St Michael's Church, Thornhill (W Yorks).

St John's Book of Revelation contains a detailed account of the events that will herald the end of the world and one of the best examples of this in any artistic medium is the principal subject of the east window of York Minster. Richard Rolle's (*c.*1300–49) version of the Last Days, described in his poem the

Pricke of Conscience is preserved in a window in All Saints, North Street, York, complete with inscriptions in English, a most unusual survival, presumably reflecting the particular requirements of the donors, who appear below (Plate 33).

Many parish churches still preserve iconographic odds and ends that attest to the variety of devotional practices in the medieval world. Devotion to the Wounds of Christ and to the Instruments of His Passion is represented at Gawsworth, Cheshire, while a particularly detailed shield of Passion Instruments can be seen in the east window of the Chapel of St John's Almshouses, Sherborne, Dorset. A Marian parallel to the Wounds of Christ can be found at Butcombe (Avon), where the Virgin's heart is shown pierced by the suffering of her Son. The late Middle Ages laid particular emphasis on the suffering of the human mother, exemplified by the *pietà* composition in which the sorrowing Virgin cradles the body of the dead Christ. Another popular devotional image in similar vein was of Christ as the 'Man of Sorrows', battered and bleeding from His final ordeal. These scenes, with their emphasis on the broken and damaged body of the Saviour, appear rather grisly to the modern eye, but they represent a significant aspect of late medieval religious life.

33   *This unusual window narrates the last days of the world as described in Richard Rolle's poem,* The Pricke of Conscience. *The English inscription explains that, on the fourteenth day, all that lives shall die: child, man and woman.*

(All Saints' Church, North Street, York, N Yorks. RCHME 1962)

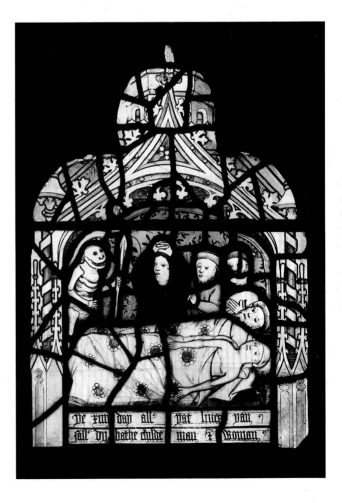

5 Humour and Horror

From the middle of the 13th century, a variety of amusing and often grotesque scenes and figures were employed by illuminators to decorate the margins of manuscripts. This development reached its apogee in the 14th century in the often riotous treatment of the borders of many East Anglian books, such as the Gorleston and Ormesby psalters.

These 'drolleries', 'babewyns' or 'grotesques' have parallels in stained glass of similar date (Plate 36). In the late 13th-century glass of Chartham (Kent), for example, a series of grotesque creatures fill round medallions. More hybrids of great imagination feature in the borders of the 14th-century glass at Stanford-on-Avon (Northants) while in the borders of the Jesse Tree at Merevale (Warwicks), strange beasts bite at their own long and sinuous necks. Very similar creatures appear in a border in Droitwich (Hereford & Worcester) and in the borders of the Latin Chapel windows of Oxford Cathedral. Creatures of this sort are not always confined to borders, however, for in the Lucy Chapel of Oxford Cathedral, New College Chapel, Oxford (Plate 35) and at Clehonger and Hadzor (both Hereford & Worcester) grotesque beasts were used to fill the otherwise awkwardly shaped tracery lights.

Although most of these bizarre creations reflect the fertile imaginations of the artists, some motifs are clearly derived from literary sources. The strange sciopod, with a single enormous foot which was used as a sun-shade, is a character from the medieval Bestiary, an encyclopaedia of animals both real and legendary (Plate 38). The pelican who, it was believed, fed her young on the blood pecked from her own breast, is another Bestiary character quite frequently found in glass.

A creature with classical connections is the centaur, shown with musical instrument in a beautiful medallion at Ringland, Norfolk. The centaur, Chiron, of Greek legend was the wisest and most learned of his kind. In Pompeian wall paintings he was drawn teaching the young Achilles to play the lyre. That this story was known to medieval artists is demonstrated by the figure of Achilles riding the centaur on the cover of the St Maurice d'Agaune ciborium (a vessel to hold the consecrated host). Could the Ringland artist also have had Chiron in mind?

A strong tradition of satire and parody runs throughout medieval art and also features in stained glass. The anti-feminism found in so much sermon literature, where it is often directed against female vanity, found an outlet in the unflatteringly contorted nude woman in one of the Christ Church, Oxford, tracery lights (Plate 34). In the same window a two-headed hybrid unites woman with that other butt of medieval irreverence, the bishop (Plate 40).

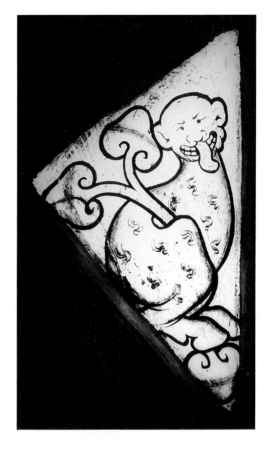

34 *(above left) A contorted and lewd figure of a woman that well illustrates an essentially anti-feminist streak that runs through so much medieval art. As the daughters of Eve, the instigator of original sin, women were held to be the weaker sex, both physically and morally.*

(Christ Church Cathedral, Oxford, Oxon. RCHME 1981)

35 *(above right) In the windows of New College Antechapel, probably glazed between 1380 and 1386, there is a rather strange contradiction between the gravity of the main light subjects and the robust treatment of the smaller tracery openings, filled with grotesque creatures such as this one.*

(New College, Oxford, Oxon. Workshop of Joan Howson, 1945–8)

36 *(right) A hybrid creature with furry hindquarters, a monstrous head and human torso, plays the cymbals in this York Minster window. Such creatures of fantasy often appear alongside scenes of a profoundly religious nature.*

(York Minster, N Yorks. North nave aisle. RCHME 1972)

37   *In a series of barbed quatrefoils set in grisaille, are a number of humorous and grotesque scenes that make the Pilgrimage Window one of the most entertaining of medieval windows.*

(York Minster, N Yorks. Pilgrimage Window. RCHME 1972)

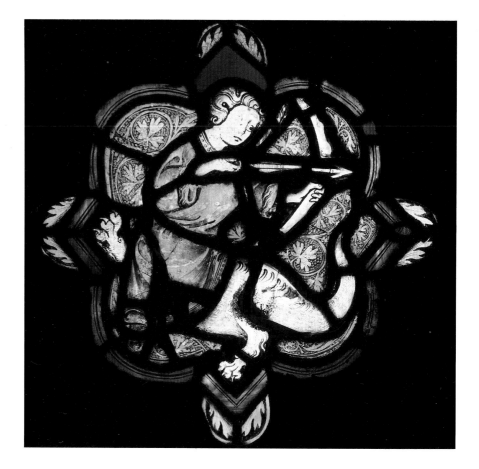

All these themes are united in the window that probably most closely resembles the page of a 14th-century illuminated manuscript, the Pilgrimage Window in the north nave aisle of York Minster. Small medallions set into the grisaille panels contain fantastic beasts, including a hybrid archer (Plate 37) and a griffin, and amusing genre scenes, one of which is devoted to a common medieval theme – the shrewish wife. In the border of the central light, that famous medieval rascal, Renard the Fox, whose escapades also unfold in manuscripts such as the Queen Mary Psalter and the Smithfield Decretals, escapes with Chantecler the Cock over his shoulder, hotly pursued by the farmer's wife brandishing a distaff. Elsewhere in the borders, monkeys perch in foliage, mimicking human activities. Some hold birds of prey on gauntleted paws (Plate 39) while others examine urine flasks, in imitation of human physicians. Across the lower borders are several scenes having close parallels in manuscript margins. Doctors are ridiculed in the scene showing two monkey physicians attending a sick ape, while the clergy is parodied in a scene showing a cock preaching from a lectern to a congregation of animals. The best known marginal scene of all from this window is undoubtedly the so-called 'Monkey's Funeral' which is, of course, a parody of the Virgin Mary's funeral. Beneath the bier, the tiny figure of the monkey with his paws stuck to the coffin can clearly be seen.

38 *This small fragment bears the sketchily drawn figure of a sciopod, who holds his enormous foot over his head.*

(York Minster, N Yorks. North nave aisle. RCHME 1972)

39 *It is perhaps the monkeys and their antics that are best remembered from the Pilgrimage Window. This little figure parodies a falconer, holding an owl on his gloved fist.*

(York Minster, N Yorks. Pilgrimage Window. RCHME 1972)

40 *In this panel, woman is joined by a bishop as the subject of derision. Anti-clerical humour may seem strange in an ecclesiastical setting but is none the less quite common in medieval art.*

(Christ Church Cathedral, Oxford, Oxon. RCHME 1981)

41 *St Martin, originally a Roman soldier, became Bishop of Tours in AD 372. The window from which this panel comes is one of the most comprehensive portrayals of his Legend in Europe, with thirteen scenes. Here St Martin compells the Devil to carry his missal.*

(Church of St Martin-le-Grand, York, N Yorks. RCHME 1966)

Glass-painters were often called upon to exert their imagination in depicting the supernatural. For medieval man, the world was beset by angels and demons, who figured prominently in the Lives of the Saints. St Anthony of Egypt was tormented by devils in the wilderness, while St Martin of Tours compelled a demon to carry his missal (Plate 41). In the Legend of St Catherine, it was a demon that suggested her tortures to the Emperor Maxentius, a detail that survives in the Peter de Dene Window in York Minster.

One of the Virgin Mary's most celebrated feats was to force the Devil to relinquish a bond acquired from the hapless monk, Theophilus. The Devil survives in two episodes from this story in Lincoln (Colour plate 11). He can appear as a somewhat ridiculous figure, but in later medieval art is often a deformed and unsightly creature, sometimes covered in fur, as at Combs (Suffolk). Elsewhere the Devil has warty skin or extra faces on stomach and buttocks (Plate 42). Some of the most fearsome manifestations of the demonic appear in illustrations of the terrors of Hell (Plate 43). The tormentors of the Damned at Fairford are amongst the most nightmarish figures in medieval art and subject the Damned to an imaginative selection of tortures.

A rare scene in the east window of York Minster which is repeated in more detail in the parish church of St Michael, Spurriergate, York, reminds us of the origin of Lucifer and his colleagues. The devils had once been angels (Lucifer means 'light-bearer'), who through arrogance and ambition, fell from grace and were expelled from Heaven. In the St Michael panel the angels are actually transformed as they fall to Hell, their feathers turning to coarse fur, their wings becoming scaly, extra faces growing on their bellies and their teeth turning to gnashing fangs.

One of the most spectacular episodes in the mystery play cycle was the enactment of the 'Harrowing of Hell', a scene quite commonly found in stained glass. Immediately before the Resurrection, Christ descends to Hell and frees from Limbo the righteous souls, having first bound Satan. The mouth of Hell was quite literally depicted as a monstrous mouth ringed with teeth, e.g. at St Kew (Cornwall) and Hengrave Hall (Suffolk) (Colour plate 8).

The medieval literature devoted to angels is copious. Not content with the relatively meagre information in the Bible, numerous writers produced complicated treatises on their nature and attributes. Nine separate orders were identified, namely Seraphim, Cherubim, Thrones, Virtues, Principalities, Dominations, Powers, Archangels and Angels, each one belonging to one of three separate hierarchies. Each Order was believed to have particular responsibilities. Seraphim and Cherubim, for example, were responsible for offering constant praise to God. The Virtues were responsible for miracles, particularly of healing, and often hold a chrismatory containing holy oils with which to anoint sufferers. A Virtue at Bolton Percy (N Yorks) anoints with a spatula of ointment the eyes of a kneeling man.

The Order of Powers was conceived as a warrior Order, responsible for fighting evil. They are often represented trampling demons underfoot as at Great Malvern Priory. At Bolton Percy the demon is restrained by a chain. In one of the Fairford windows, a group of these warrior angels is engaged in an aerial battle with a group of demons. It was also commonly believed that each Order had particular responsibility for an order of humanity. Two angels surviving from a series at Ufford in Suffolk confirm this, one bearing an inscription linking the Dominations with earthly emperors and kings, while the other links Virtues with the orders of priests and religious.

43   *In a remarkable panel of 15th-century fragments, the Torments of Hell are vividly depicted. The Damned, including a queen, a bishop and a pope, are trundled off to torture by two pointed-eared demons. In the foreground, a tonsured priest weeps at his fate.*

(Church of St Mary, Ticehurst, E Sussex. C. Dalton 1975)

42   *The glass-painter here portrays the Devil as a hairy creature, with prominent teeth and talons and extra disfiguring faces growing on his knees and belly.*

(York Minster, N Yorks. St Cuthbert Window. RCHME 1971)

44   *In this beautiful late 15th-century panel the Archangel Gabriel appears in his most common role, as the bearer of the glad Annunciation tidings.*

(Church of St Peter and St Paul, East Harling, Norfolk. D King 1947–8)

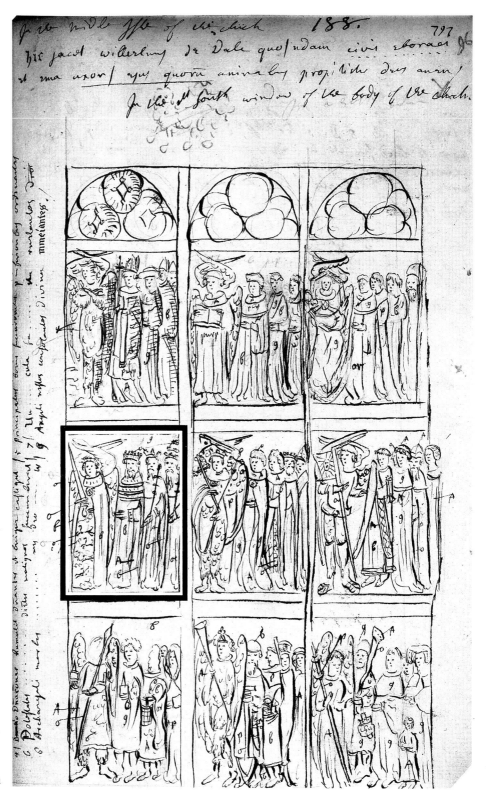

a

45 *In 1965 a remarkable reconstruction of a lost window was undertaken on the strength of a drawing in the Bodleian Library. Henry Johnston's drawing of 1670 (**a**) had been made when the window was all but complete, and the accuracy of his record, (which included transcriptions of inscriptions and notes on the colour of the glass), together with the obvious iconographic interest of the window, made this task an exciting challenge. Even in this restored panel, the Order of Dominations, (**b**) the superb quality of the work can be appreciated.*

(All Saints' Church, North Street, York, N Yorks. RCHME 1964 and 1966)

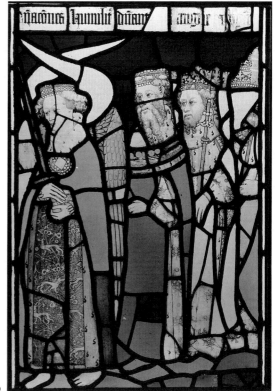

b

A fascinating window devoted to the Orders of Angels survives in a heavily restored condition in All Saints, North Street, York. Each Order is shown leading a procession of mortals of the appropriate social rank. The window survived more or less intact until the 18th century, having been recorded in great detail in 1670 by the antiquarian Henry Johnston. By the 19th century, however, it had been reduced to a jumble of fragments and in this state was interpreted as the remains of a Corpus Christi procession and as the Coronation procession of Edward IV in York in 1464. The rediscovery of Henry Johnston's drawing in the Bodleian Library enabled the window to be reconstructed in 1965 (Plate 45).

The names of four individual archangels, whose job was to convey to humanity messages of special importance, were known through biblical and apocryphal texts. Gabriel is perhaps the best known, having been entrusted with the Annunciation message to the Virgin Mary (Plate 44). Michael is also well known, often depicted fighting a dragon or weighing souls at the Last Judgement, as at Martham (Norfolk) where the devils try to tip the balance. Raphael was known from the apocryphal books of Enoch and Tobit. His name means 'God has healed' and in the story of Tobit he enables Tobias to heal Tobit's blindness. The fourth archangel, Uriel, is very rarely represented in glass, although he was probably included in Great Malvern Priory and survives heavily restored at Kingsland (Hereford & Worcester).

In anonymous form, angels abound in stained glass, being a particularly popular subject in tracery lights. Sometimes they are dressed in the alb or

46   *(right) This fine 15th-century panel is a fortunate survivor from the bombed medieval cathedral in Coventry. The angel is feathered, with two pairs of wings and wears a scarf and cross diadem on its head. It stands on a wheel, described in the Prophet Ezekiel's vision of God's chariot supported by Cherubim.*

(St Michael's Hall, Coventry, W Midlands. RCHME 1981)

47   *(far right) One of the most important duties of an angel was to offer praise to God. This rather fragmented figure holds a medieval version of the bagpipes under one arm.*

(Guildhall, Norwich, Norfolk. E.C. Le Grice 1946)

dalmatic of the deacon, but are also commonly covered entirely in feathers that end at their wrists, ankles and neck (Plate 46). This dress, if that is what it can be called, closely resembles the feathered costumes worn by the actors in the Mystery plays.

Angels commonly carry shields of arms and sometimes support the Instruments of Christ's Passion (e.g. Rendcomb, Glos). In their role of praising God, they are often shown swinging censers (for example, at Dilwyn, Hereford & Worcester) or are depicted as musicians. At Barkway (Herts), they play harp and kettle drums; at Lincoln, mandora and gittern. Angel musicians appear to have been particularly popular in Norfolk – a gittern is played at Hale, a shawm at Guestwick, a psaltery at North Elmham and bagpipes at Sustead and Norwich Guildhall (Plate 47). Perhaps the most extensive surviving angelic orchestra is the one in the tracery of the east window of the Beauchamp Chapel, Warwick, where a fascinating variety of medieval instruments is represented.

6 Glimpses of Medieval Life

The largest surviving quantity of painted glass in England is to be found in religious settings and is devoted to the depiction of a religious and spiritual narrative. None the less, it is sometimes possible to catch glimpses of the everyday medieval world familiar to the glass-painters who, in ignorance of the fashions of the distant past, often drew upon contemporary life in their portrayal of historical events. Stained glass is a particularly valuable source of information for the study of medieval dress. Donor portraits are often the most detailed, although confined to the higher levels of society, and unlike monumental brasses, for example, show costume in colour.

The dress of the 13th century and early 14th century for both men and women was not dissimilar. For both sexes, garments tended to be loose fitting and in three main parts: tunic, over-tunic (*supertunica*) with wider sleeves, and mantle. Only the shape of the neckline and length of the skirt differed to any degree. The looseness of the fit arose from the custom of cutting garments in a basic T-shape, to which was added a skirt and sleeves sewn on at the elbow. The fabric of the lower sleeve would then be wound around the arm and fastened in place every time the garment was put on. The upper sleeve remained baggy. Uncomplicated garments of this type required no special fastenings and could be pulled on over the head.

All these features can be seen quite clearly in the windows of the choir of Canterbury Cathedral (Plate 48). Both men and women wear simple belted tunics. The shorter garments of the men are sometimes worn over baggy trousers or leggings covering the ankles and tops of the shoes, or buskins, as in the scene of the Magi before King Herod, where spurs can also be seen. Poorer men are often shown bare-legged, for example, the workmen who witness the burial of William of Gloucester. The baggy underpants that were worn beneath the tunic can be discerned, for example, in the scene of the castration of Eilward of Westoning.

The Canterbury panel of the Israelites departing from Egypt illustrates the female costume of long, tight-sleeved tunic worn under a supertunica with shorter, wider sleeves. The Israelite women also wear the commonest female head covering of the period, a veil with the ends wound round the neck and breast like a scarf. The figures in the later Lincoln Cathedral panels wear very similar apparel, although the men tend to wear longer tunics.

By 1350, English fashion had undergone some violent changes that did not go unnoticed, or indeed uncriticized, by contemporaries. Most importantly perhaps, the tunic and supertunica became tighter fitting, as a result of new methods of cutting cloth. Sleeves were now set into round openings at

48   *All three Magi shown here wear the most common elements of male dress found in the Canterbury glass. The belted tunic is worn over leggings that hang loosely over soft slipper-like shoes. On the outstretched arm of the central figure the way in which the baggy sleeves were wound around the forearm is clearly visible. This panel also illustrates the monumental quality of the animal painting at Canterbury. Back-painting has been skilfully applied to the horse's flank to give a naturalistic effect.*

(Canterbury Cathedral, Kent. Choir ambulatory. RCHME 1962)

1 *In his* History of the Abbots, *Bede describes how in* AD *674, Abbot Benedict Biscop invited Frankish glaziers to England to glaze his new stone churches at Monkwearmouth and Jarrow, such knowledge having been lost in England. Excavated fragments like these reveal that these early windows consisted of unpainted pieces leaded into patterns and possibly outline shapes of figures. The glass itself has the high soda content typical of Roman glass, and so is extremely durable. Thus, after centuries underground, it retains its bright colour and translucency.*

(Church of St Paul, Jarrow, Tyne & Wear. RCHME 1980)

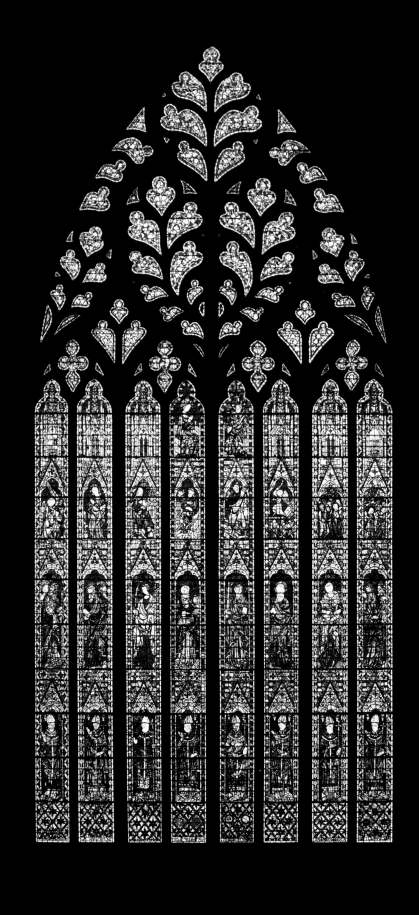

2   (left) The west window of York Minster represents one of the masterpieces of English
medieval glass-painting. In February 1339, Archbishop Melton gave 100 marks for the
glazing of the west window of the recently completed nave. His personal wishes are surely
revealed in the subject matter. Eight of his illustrious predecessors are commemorated
beneath figures of the apostles. Its use of canopies and alternating layers of deep colour and
lighter glass make it one of the best expressions of the 14th-century approach to window
design.

(York Minster, N Yorks. West window. RCHME 1967)

3   (above) A panel depicting the Virgin and Child in Warndon Parish Church is the work of
a group of glass-painters working in the Worcester area in the early decades of the 14th
century. An almost identical group survives at nearby Fladbury. The rich leafy green was one
of the favourite colours of glass-painters of the period.

(Warndon Parish Church, Hereford & Worcester. RCHME 1985)

4   (left) An accomplished panel of c.1350, depicting Joachim in the wilderness, displays both the versatility of yellow stain, which can clearly be seen in the fine detail of the border of his hood, and also its wide range of colour tones. Throughout the panel the artist has used a variety of painted detail and delicate stickwork.

(York Minster, N Yorks. Nave aisle. RCHME 1972)

5   (right) An early 15th-century figure of St Lawrence, formerly in the Chapel of Hampton Court (Hereford & Worcester), and now in the V & A, displays the palette typical of so much 15th-century glass. Apart from the red and blue pot-metal glasses, the most dominant colour is the yellow stain, applied liberally to the white glass. The inscription that identifies the saint is in abbreviated black-letter script: S[an]c[tu]s Laurencius.

(Victoria & Albert Museum. RCHME 1982)

6   This striking head from the Crucifixion Window at King's College Chapel demonstrates the startling degree of realism achieved by the foreign glass-painters employed by the Crown in the first third of the 16th century.

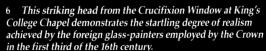

(King's College Chapel, Cambridge, Cambs. H. Wayment c.1972)

7   Beneath the figure, an inscription in French asks for our prayers for Vincent, who is portrayed above, offering a model of his window to the Virgin and Child in the adjoining light. The main lights contain a series of martyrdoms, including that of St Vincent.

8   In an exceptionally well preserved early 16th-century window in the Chapel of Hengrave Hall, a cycle of scenes from the Creation to the Last Judgement unfolds in vivid colours. Individual lights often contain more than one element of the narrative, as here, where six scenes from Christ's Passion fill only three lights. Being in a private house, the window escaped the attentions of iconoclasts and very little original glass required replacement when it was restored in 1898.

(Hengrave Hall Chapel, Hengrave, Suffolk. RCHME 1984)

is located in the east window of a small parish church. However, it is a church in which the medieval bishops of Hereford once worshipped, which no doubt accounts for the remarkable quality of the stained glass, with its fine painted detail and rich palette.

(Church of St Michael, Eaton Bishop, Hereford and Worcester. RCHME 1986)

10   *(right)* This panel portrays the Archangel Michael in one of his guises, as slayer of the dragon (Rev 12:7–9). This figure is a good example of the vigorously realistic style of the early 16th century, and is in remarkably good condition. The medieval chapel at Balliol has been replaced by a 19th-century building in which the medieval stained glass has been reset, not without casualty.

(Balliol College Chapel, Oxford, Oxon, RCHME 1986)

11   In this panel from Lincoln Cathedral (c.1230), the Virgin Mary, labelled in Lombardic capitals 'S[ancta] Maria', is seen retrieving Theophilus's bond from the Devil. To the left, Theophilus is seen handing it to his bishop. Note how a piece of streaky flashed ruby glass has been used to good effect for the Devil's head.

(Lincoln Cathedral, Lincs. North choir aisle. RCHME 1984)

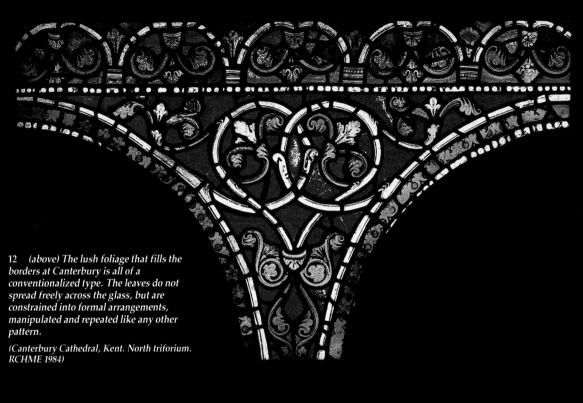

12   (above) The lush foliage that fills the borders at Canterbury is all of a conventionalized type. The leaves do not spread freely across the glass, but are constrained into formal arrangements, manipulated and repeated like any other pattern.

(Canterbury Cathedral, Kent. North triforium. RCHME 1984)

13   (below) It would seem that the 15th-century glass-painter responsible for this zodiac roundel had never seen a crab, the cancerian symbol.

(Church of St Mary, Shrewsbury, Shropshire. RCHME 1985)

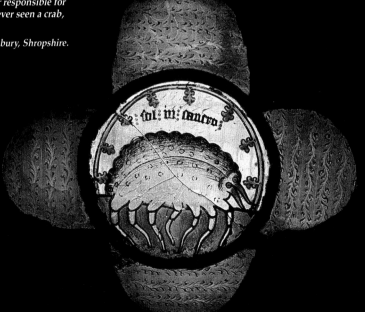

14 *The medieval parish church of Twycross is distinguished by its remarkable collection of Continental stained glass, which includes panels like this one, of the Presentation of Christ in the Temple, from the Lady Chapel of Abbot Suger's Abbey Church of St Denis near Paris, dating from c.1145.*

(Church of St Mary, Twycross, Leics. RCHME 1985)

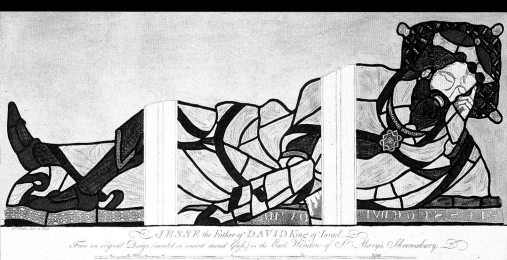

JESSE the Father of DAVID King of Israel.
From an original Design (executed in ancient stained Glass) in the East Window of S.t Mary's Shrewsbury.

15 *William Fowler (1761–1832) drew his first antiquarian subject in 1796. Although he is perhaps best known for his drawings of Roman mosaic pavements, he was also one of the earliest antiquarians to record stained glass with care and considerable accuracy, noting for example, the position of the leads. His first glass subject is dated 1802 and this figure of Jesse from St Mary's, Shrewsbury (Shrops) was issued in his first series of engravings offered for sale on 1 October 1804.*

(Collection of the Society of Antiquaries, London)

49 *This 14th-century lady wears the tighter-sleeved tunic with bell-sleeved supertunica, together with wimple and crespine (a type of hair-net) that can just be seen under her veil.*

(Church of St Mary, Waterperry, Oxon. RCHME 1972)

shoulder level, making possible a more slender outline around the torso. Sleeves were cut to be tighter fitting and garments could no longer simply be pulled over the head. Buttoned or laced openings were necessary. The sleeves of the supertunica were cut into a wide bell shape and often hung in exaggerated strips from the elbow. This combination of tighter under-garments and loose-sleeved outer gown can clearly be seen on the anonymous lady at Waterperry (Oxon) (Plate 49). The rather mannered contours of male attire of the period included a low-waisted tunic, often worn indecently short, which was padded around the belly and chest to give an unnaturally serpentine outline to the body that could be enhanced by a heavy, low-slung belt.

Elaborate hats for men do not appear to have been popular until the second half of the 14th century, but female head-dresses often appear in fascinating detail in stained glass. From the last quarter of the 13th century, hair was confined in a net or crespine, clearly visible in the Penancer's Window in York Minster. Only young unmarried girls would wear their hair long and loose. The most commonly represented head covering is the wimple, a kerchief enveloping the neck and breast and fastened at the sides of the head. When worn with a veil, only a small portion of the face remained visible (Plate 49).

The wimple was particularly popular with older women and remained the standard for widows, even when it had ceased to be worn by other women.

As the illustrating of contemporary dress became more detailed in the 15th century, so did the variety of head-dress to be found in stained glass of the period. The popular butterfly head-dress is worn by the ladies at Long Melford (Suffolk), where the late 15th-century fashion for shaving the forehead can also be seen (Plate 51), a feature also visible on the figure of Elizabeth Woodville in the Royal Window at Canterbury. St Anne in All Souls College Chapel, Oxford wears a modestly wired head-dress, but more extravagant horned versions were also popular. Although preachers attacked them vehemently as a sign of excessive feminine vanity and the work of the Devil, the Virgin is wearing one in the east window of Holy Trinity, Goodramgate, York (Plate 22).

Male fashions also began to display elements of extravagance. Tunics were worn short to reveal coloured tights (Plate 53) and a variety of often exotic hats became fashionable (Plate 50). Everywhere, one is conscious of the increasingly rich range of fabrics available. Fur lines the vestments of a bishop at Stratton-on-the-Fosse (Somerset), jewels decorate the hems of the angels' robes in St Martin's, Stamford (Lincs) and ermine edges an exquisite brocade in the Angels Window in All Saints, North Street, York. The same window also contains one of the earliest illustrations of spectacles.

50   *This detail from the St William Window illustrates the sumptuous sort of head-dress that was popular among the wealthy merchant class of 15th-century York. In this case it was lined with ermine, which is clearly identified by the black tail-tips.*

(York Minster, N Yorks. St William Window. RCHME 1971)

51 *The parish church at Long Melford was rebuilt c.1460 to c.1495 by a group of wealthy parishioners whose names are recorded in inscriptions in the stonework and in the stained glass of the windows. Anne Crane wears the dress appropriate to a lady of substance; her gown is trimmed with fur, at her throat is a fine necklace and on her head is an elaborate 'butterfly' head-dress through which her shaven forehead can be seen.*

(Holy Trinity Church, Long Melford, Suffolk. C. Woodforde c.1950)

52 *In this fascinating scene, the young Virgin Mary visits her cousin Elizabeth, soon to give birth to St John the Baptist. As she raises her hands in greeting and recognition of the Virgin and the unborn Saviour, Elizabeth reveals the laced front of her own maternity dress.*

(Church of St Peter and St Paul, East Harling, Norfolk. D. King 1947–8)

53 *(left) The rather outlandish nature of later 15th-century fashions is illustrated in this panel in Norwich. St Peter is brought before the Emperor Nero, who wears a short, flared tunic with fur trim and bell-collar. Coloured tights emphasize the legs.*

(Church of St Peter Mancroft, Norwich, Norfolk. D. King 1947).

54 *(right) In this late 15th-century window Edmund Rich (c.1175–1240), Archbishop of Canterbury, canonized in 1246, wears the vestments appropriate to his rank. He holds the cross staff of office and wears white alb and fringed dalmatic under a richly decorated chasuble. Around his shoulders and down the front of his vestments hangs the pallium of white wool decorated with crosses granted to archbishops by the Pope himself.*

(Great Malvern Priory, Hereford & Worcester. S. Pitcher c.1936)

55   *The Chapel of the Vyne has been described as 'the best late medieval private chapel in England' (Sir Nikolaus Pevsner) and its glass befits this status. The house and chapel belonged to Lord Sandys, Lord Chamberlain to Henry VIII. Henry visited the house in person in 1516. The King, Queen Katherine of Aragon and Queen Margaret of Scotland (Henry's sister) are all commemorated in the glass, each accompanied by their patron saint. Here, Margaret is shown in the sumptuous fashion of the first quarter of the 16th century, accompanied by her name saint, who emerges from the belly of a fearsome dragon.*

(Chapel of the Vyne, Sherborne St John, Hants. S. Pitcher c.1925)

This interest in contemporary fashions of the 15th century even extended to the depiction of maternity wear. In the east windows of St Peter Mancroft, Norwich and St Peter and St Paul, East Harling (Norfolk), St Elizabeth is shown in a dress with laced front that accommodates her swollen stomach (Plate 52).

Surviving early 16th-century glass similarly provides ample evidence of contemporary fashion, one of the major innovations of the period being the habit of slashing parts of the outer garments, especially sleeves, to reveal the fabric worn below. Pedimental head-dresses favoured by the ladies of the period abound in the glass of King's College Chapel (Cambs) but at Fairford these have in some cases been supplanted by the elaborate head-dresses fashionable on the Continent. Some impression of the richness of royal dress of the day can be gleaned from the glass in the Chapel of the Vyne, Sherborne St John (Hants); Henry VIII, Katherine of Aragon, and Margaret of Scotland (Plate 55), are all represented and wear richly furred and trimmed clothes; the Mary Magdalene at the foot of the cross also displaying the fashion for slashed sleeves.

56   *The profession of these three figures is made clear by their distinctive dress. The medieval judge traditionally wore a long plain gown lined with vair, a variegated fur derived from squirrels, and a coif of white silk or linen.*

(Holy Trinity Church, Long Melford, Suffolk. C. Woodforde c.1950)

Stained glass also provides useful information about the appearance of medieval vestments (Plate 54). Apart from the numerous representations of episcopal and arch-episcopal vestments, deacons in striped dalmatics (York Minster, north choir aisle), cardinals in crimson (St Jerome in St John's Church, Cirencester, Glos), popes in triple tiaras (Plate 25), abbesses in veils and wimples (Merton College Chapel, Oxford), parish priests in simple gowns (Plate 19) and even doctors of canon law (St Michael's Church, Eaton Bishop, Hereford & Worcester) can all be found.

The evidence for the appearance of the professional classes is perhaps less common in stained glass than it is in memorial brasses, although at Holy Trinity Church, Long Melford (Suffolk) legal dress is clearly shown (Plate 56).

The evolution of medieval armour also unfolds in windows, although it is dangerous to attempt to date stained glass by the style of the armour, as the simplest styles of protective dress were current over a long period (Plate 57). By the late 13th century, leather and metal plates had been added to this basic protection and can be seen on an early 14th-century kneeling donor figure at Lowick, Northants (Plate 58).

57   *For the protagonists in the siege of Canterbury, plundered by the Danes in 1011, the principal protection was afforded by a shirt of chain mail that covered the head but left the legs bare. Additional protection was provided by the conical helmet and kite-shaped shield.*

(Canterbury Cathedral, Kent. North triforium. RCHME 1984)

58   *(above) In the early 14th century, metal or leather plates were added to the chain mail at its most vulnerable points. Sir Simon de Drayton, seen here offering a model of the church he beautified, wears them on his knees, elbows and shoulders.*

(Church of St Peter, Lowick, Northants. RCHME 1982)

59   *(right) This figure of a knight of the Ruyhale family illustrates some of the features of late 14th- and early 15th-century armour. The pointed bascinet (helmet) with raised visor is laced to the aventail (the mail around the neck and shoulders). The rerebrace, which protects the upper arm, and the vambrace covering the forearm are also visible. Cuisses (thigh armour) and jambes (lower leg armour) cover the legs. The tighter fitting breastplate mirrors the shapes favoured in civilian male attire.*

(Church of St Peter and St Paul, Birtsmorton, Hereford & Worcester. S. Pitcher c.1925)

Plate armour gradually emerged as the principal form of protection, covering hands and feet by the end of the 14th century as in the figure of Sir James Berners, West Horsley, Surrey; and eventually encasing the head as well (Plate 59). A heraldic surcoat was often worn over the armour, as on the eight figures of kings in St Mary's Hall, Coventry (W Midlands). The image of St George slaying the dragon afforded the glass-painter the opportunity to paint armour in action, as at North Tuddenham, (Norfolk), where St George appears as a mounted knight who vigorously spears a beast writhing at the horse's feet. By the end of the 15th century, some of the best armour was influenced by Continental design. The three armoured figures in St Bartholomew's Church, Ripponden (W Yorks), provide a good example of the highly decorative, not to say exotic, impression that this could convey.

Some of the most fascinating insights into the everyday life and customs of ordinary medieval society can be gained from roundels of the Labours of the Months, mostly 15th century in date and showing the seasonal occupations of rural society. These scenes, paralleled in manuscript calendars, reveal the preoccupations of the majority of men and women. As the year unfolds, each seasonal task is depicted in turn. The early months of the year were devoted to such tasks as pruning, shown in the March roundel in Lincoln Cathedral. The activity in the fields increased in the summer and early autumn months as the crops ripened and were harvested (Plate 60). Two 14th-century survivals in All Saints' Church, Dewsbury (W Yorks) portray harvesting and threshing. An example now in the Victoria & Albert Museum, but formerly at Cassiobury Park (Herts), has a valuable view of a medieval harrow in the roundel for October.

At the end of a year of hard work, the medieval farmer could look forward to the festive season. The November roundels from Matfield House (Kent), Dewsbury (W Yorks) and Besthorpe (Norfolk) all show the slaughter of a pig and Cassiobury's December a scene of feasting.

These small panels also demonstrate the importance of women in the rural economy. A fine, coloured medallion at Brandiston Hall (Norfolk) shows a woman wielding a scythe, and the Cassiobury roundels for July and August both show women working alongside their men. A second Brandiston piece reveals an aspect of English rural life that appears almost foreign to modern eyes: a man harvesting grapes, reminding us that wine was still produced in quantity in medieval England.

Urban-based occupations appear less frequently, although in a tracery panel from Helmdon (Northants) a stonemason is shown at work. In the west window of St George's Chapel, Windsor, is a rare portrait of a master mason, either Henry Janyns or William Vertue, who completed the chancel vaults between 1506 and 1511 (Plate 62). Until the restorations of the 19th century, the east window of Winchester College Chapel contained contemporary portraits of William Winford, the master mason, an anonymous carpenter, Simon Membury, the clerk of works and Thomas of Oxford, the master glazier, in addition to William of Wykeham, Edward III and his grandson, Richard II. Fully fledged trade scenes such as those in Chartres Cathedral and the Collegiate Church of Semer-en-Auxois are rare in England. A notable exception is to be found in York Minster, where in addition to the bell-founding scenes in Richard Tunnoc's window, two scenes in the north nave clerestory depict the activities of a wine merchant (Plate 63).

The occasional glimpse of the medieval domestic interior can also be seen. A

60   *Three 15th-century roundels showing the rural occupations of some of the busiest months of the year. In the July roundel, (**a**) the man wields a scythe and in August (**b**) the woman is using a sickle. The man in the September roundel (**c**) employs a flail to thresh the harvested crop. Tools of similar design continued in use until the early part of this century.*

(July and August from Cassiobury Park, Watford, Herts, now both in the Victoria & Albert Museum. September from St Mary's Hall, Coventry, W Midlands. RCHME 1982 and S. Pitcher c.1925)

61   *The Birth of the Virgin has afforded the glass-painter the opportunity to show details of a medieval domestic interior. St Anne lies in a canopied four-poster, while the infant Virgin rests in a cradle, securely laced in as she is gently rocked by two angels. A tub chair rests on the tiled floor and St Anne is attended by smartly dressed midwives.*

(Leicester Museum, Leics. S. Pitcher undated)

roundel of February from St Michael Coslany, Norwich (Norfolk), now in the Burrell collection in Glasgow, illustrates a man warming his feet at his hearth. A pot simmers on the fire, a towel hangs on a rail and on the mantle rests a jug and plate. A fragment of what was once a similar scene in St Mary's Hall, Coventry (W Midlands), includes a side of bacon hanging from a hook.

The furnishings to be found in a well-to-do medieval bedroom can be seen at Great Malvern Priory, in the panel of the birth of the Virgin, where St Anne sits in a bed enclosed by rich hangings. Tub-shaped armchairs also appear to have been common in the bedroom, appearing in the Nativity scene at St Peter Mancroft, Norwich, in All Saints, North Street, York and in a roundel in Leicester Museum (Plate 61).

62   *(left) This master mason of the early 16th century wears the heavy fur-trimmed gown and blunt-toed shoes that became fashionable in Tudor times. Men favoured a broad, massive outline and gowns were worn short to show off the legs. Although portraits of artists and craftsmen are rare in the Middle Ages, their more frequent appearance from the late 14th century onwards reflects the growing esteem in which these men were held.*

(St George's Chapel, Windsor Castle, Windsor, Berks. S. Pitcher 1945)

63   *(above) A rare trade scene showing the wine merchant offering his wares to a client 'Pur cink mars' (for five marks). The price was clearly acceptable, for in a companion panel money is shown changing hands.*

(York Minster, N Yorks. Nave clerestory. RCHME 1978)

Another Leicester roundel, of the Sacrament of Extreme Unction shows a sorrowing woman at the bedside of her dying husband, and reminds us that in an age with a very rudimentary medical knowledge, premature death was common. The terror on the faces of the plague-stricken Fitz Eisulf household, in one of the Canterbury Becket windows, illustrates very vividly the vulnerability of medieval society in the face of contagious diseases. Uroscopic examination was a principal means of diagnosis and so it is a urine flask that is being examined by St Cosmas (or St Damian) at Minster Lovell (Oxon). Little wonder that it was to the saints as much as to the doctors that people turned in time of infirmity. St Apollonia's help was sought for the relief of toothache and St Margaret's protection was sought by women in childbirth.

64   *Three panels in the Canterbury glass are devoted to the story of Mathilda of Cologne, a madwoman who had committed murder. A vision prompted her to travel to Becket's shrine, where a cure was effected. In this scene she is brutally treated by attendants, the violence of events being emphasized by the fluttering draperies.*

(Canterbury Cathedral, Kent. Trinity Chapel ambulatory. RCHME 1985)

It was the great pilgrim centres that offered the faithful the most hope, however. The representations of St William's shrine in the St William Window at York provide one of the best glimpses of the pilgrim traffic. A group of sick and lame men and women is shown bathing in the water at the shrine, which is adorned with models of those parts of the body for which cures had been sought.

It was Canterbury and the shrine of Becket that exerted the greatest pull throughout the Middle Ages. In his *Canterbury Tales*, Chaucer has left an amusing picture of the variety of people who made the journey, seeking physical and spiritual benefit. All conditions of men and women are pictured in the Miracle windows in the Cathedral, which were designed to encourage and edify the pilgrim as he made his way towards the shrine itself. The boundaries between physical and spiritual sickness were often blurred and some illnesses were considered to be the result of demonic possession. Mental illnesses certainly fell into this category and the mad woman Mathilda of Cologne is shown being roughly treated before her cure at Becket's shrine (Plate 64).

The milestones in the progress of life from birth to death are marked by the Sacraments of the Church and in the 15th century the Seven Sacraments became a popular subject in glass, often, as at Melbury Bubb (Dorset), linked

65   *In the parish church of Doddiscombsleigh, depictions of all Seven Sacraments survive. In this scene of matrimony, the young man, guided by the priest, slips a ring on to the bride's finger, although of her right hand, while family and friends look on.*

(Church of St Michael, Doddiscombsleigh, Devon. S. Pitcher c.1920)

66   *The glass-painter was sometimes called upon to portray grave-clothes.*

(York Minster, N Yorks. Great East Window. RCHME 1970)

to a central image of the body of Christ by streams of blood flowing from his wounds. All seven (Baptism, Confirmation, Eucharist, Matrimony, Penance, Holy Orders and Extreme Unction) can be seen at Doddiscombsleigh (Devon), although the central figure of Christ dates from the 19th century.

These medieval scenes serve as a reminder that many of the customs associated with these occasions today are rooted in much older practice. The baptized child held naked over the font at Tattershall (Lincs) is accompanied by his sponsors as well as his parents, much as one might expect of godparents today. The child to be confirmed, however, was clearly much younger than is now usual, being still a babe in arms, and in another of the Leicester Museum roundels is shown wrapped in swaddling. Representations of the Sacrament of Matrimony contain all those elements that are a familiar part of the service today (Plate 65).

Even the shroud in its various forms can be found in stained glass. In the Resurrection scenes in Wells Cathedral choir and in the east window of Carlisle Cathedral, the shroud is a loose cloth that flaps about the figures, while in the Wells Chapter House it appears as a long bag with an opening down the front. Elsewhere it appears in yet another form, gathered and knotted at the top of the head, as frequently also shown on memorial brasses (Plate 66).

7 The Natural World

Although so much stained glass is devoted to the religious and spiritual world, the medium also abounds with observations of the natural world, sometimes in a remarkably lively manner. The way in which naturalized foliage forms were gradually adopted in stained glass in the course of the late 13th and early 14th centuries has already been mentioned. It is, however, in some of the earliest windows that the first vivid glimpses of the natural world can be seen, produced by artists working in the closing years of the 12th century.

The 12th century witnessed a revival of interest in the classical past. In some parts of Europe, in Italy and France in particular, physical evidence of a Roman heritage remained to be studied. The Bishop of Winchester, Henry Blois, even collected pieces of Roman sculpture when on a visit to Rome in 1151 and brought them home to England. One can imagine the impact that these noble and technically advanced works must have had on the medieval artist. Throughout late 12th-century Europe, artists in all media were briefly influenced by this brush with the classical past and produced works with a remarkably monumental quality and emotional power. Glass-painters were not immune to this influence and some of the late 12th-century Canterbury masters, working in the Canterbury choir, displayed a marked interest in anatomy. The figure of Adam, for example, has a strongly delineated torso, which, although not strictly accurate, is none the less extremely effective in marked contrast to the conventionalized tree on which he hangs his adze (Plate 67).

This anatomical interest extended to the depiction of the Canterbury animals. Horses in particular are portrayed as noble beasts with fine heads and powerful bodies (Plate 48). A more exotic creature appears in the scene of the visit of the Queen of Sheba, where her attendants, given clearly negroid features, ride what are surely supposed to be camels. News of the strange creatures of the east no doubt filtered back with returning crusaders. Another panel has more mundane creatures as in the scene of the boy drowned while stoning frogs. The frogs, all drawn from the same cartoon, leap in great alarm as they are pelted with stones thrown from the river bank. The foliage filling the borders, however, remains conventionalized (Colour plate 12).

For the glass-painters of the 14th century, the natural world was a source of decorative inspiration. The real world was constantly overrun by creatures of the imagination, so that squirrels, monkeys and birds are often seen alongside griffins and centaurs. The Jesse tree with its lush vine foliage was, however, a more appropriate setting for real birds and animals, although at Merevale

67 *This figure, originally positioned in the clerestory, displays a vigour and strength which characterizes the work of some of the earliest Canterbury masters. The partially clad Adam offered the artist an unusual opportunity to depict the human body. Note also the hooves that are still attached to Adam's fur apron.*

(Canterbury Cathedral, Kent. Future position uncertain. RCHME 1973)

68   *In this 14th-century panel, the natural world has provided inspiration for all but the heraldry. Naturally curling foliage decorates the grisaille, while birds and squirrels fill the oak trails in the borders.*

(All Saints' Church, Ryther, N Yorks. RCHME 1976)

(Warwicks), animals and birds (including an owl) inhabit the vine, while grotesques occupy the borders. It is in the depiction of foliage that the glass-painters of the 14th and 15th century excelled themselves. Although the Five Sisters Window in York Minster, of mid 13th-century date, was already beginning to display natural elements in its foliage grisaille, it was only in the 1280s and 1290s that recognizable leaf forms began to appear, in some cases still leaded into the geometric patterns favoured in earlier decades. By the time the Chapter House vestibule of York Minster was glazed in the 1290s, naturalized leaf forms had even made their way into the borders. At Bredon (Hereford & Worcester), oak and maple are entwined through a trellis in the early 14th-century grisaille. Less costly schemes would use identical quarries with a simple repeated design (Plate 49).

Some of the loveliest leaf forms are to be found in background diapers. The west window of York Minster uses five different patterns, all based on foliage, although adapted by the artists' decorative imaginations. One of the most common 15th-century background patterns has even been termed 'the seaweed diaper' because of its similarity to bladder-wrack seaweed. The 15th-century glass-painters of Norwich favoured a border in which foliage wrapped itself around a pole.

Animals and birds can also be used as a purely decorative motif, as adaptable as any other form of pattern (Plate 68). At Aldwincle (Northants), the motif of a hound pursuing a hare has been turned into a never-ending chase around the borders. One of the favourite devices of a group of late 15th-century artists working in the Stamford and Peterborough area was the use of small birds and lions in the niches of the canopy side-shafts (Plates 24 and 25).

In the 15th and 16th centuries naturalism was replaced by increasing realism, particularly in the realization of landscapes. The catalyst was a growing awareness of space and its implications. In the early 14th century, Italian artists such as Duccio and Giotto had begun to experiment with space, setting their figures in believable spatial settings. In the late 14th century, artists north of the Alps also began to develop this aspect of painting, seeking to portray the third dimension in their work. In late 14th- and 15th-century France, manuscript illuminators, some from the Low Countries, began to paint landscapes of astonishing realism. In English glass-painting this interest was relatively slow to assert itself, although some of the 15th-century Labours of the Months roundels do depict rudimentary landscapes with great vigour and humour (Plate 60). Mention should also be made, however, of a much earlier landscape created by an artist for whom the concept of perspective would have had very little meaning. One of the late 12th-century Canterbury masters in his scenes from the parable of the sower, produced a landscape of remarkable simplicity and impact. Using strips of different coloured glass arranged diagonally across his panel, he created the effect of a gently receding field on which his sower performs his tasks (Plate 70).

Even in the 15th century, however, there was a tendency for the distinction between the real world and legendary worlds to be blurred. At Ewelme in Oxfordshire, for example, the yale and the unicorn appear alongside the lion and the white hind. Of course, in an age when knowledge of foreign lands came from highly colourful accounts such as *Sir John de Mandeville's Travels*, the legendary unicorn sounded no more bizarre than the elephant or giraffe.

69   *Tucked away in the corner of a Fairford window is this view into a receding landscape of fields, rivers and spires. The eye is drawn under the painted arch to a hazy and long-lost world. Although this is only a small area within the window, the detail is meticulously painted. There is a rowing-boat on the river and, in the middle of the scene, a tiny windmill on a hill.*

(Church of St Mary, Fairford, Glos. RCHME 1972)

70   *This late 12th-century landscape manages to convey a sense of space in an age prior to the understanding of the rules of perspective. Its freshness and vitality give it an extraordinary power.*

(Canterbury Cathedral, Kent. North choir aisle. RCHME 1985)

At this time, birds and animals were rendered with increasing care (Plate 71). This is clearly shown in panels such as the Creation scene at Great Malvern Priory where a hedgehog is one of the more familiar beasts at the feet of the Creator. There was also a noticeable revival of interest in the anatomy of the human form. In the great east window of York Minster the naked Adam and Eve are accurately drawn, although Eve is given the slightly distended abdomen that conformed to contemporary ideals of female beauty.

It is most unlikely that 15th-century glass-painters would have drawn every figure directly from life. Even in an age when greater realism was prized, the use of the pattern book continued to dominate the workshop although the strange inaccuracies that appear in the less familiar creatures show that artistic licence was sometimes required (Colour plate 13). The beautiful Pepysian sketchbook at Magdalene College, Cambridge contains exquisite drawings of birds and animals probably intended to serve as models for members of a painter's workshop.

It was not until the early 16th century, however, that there was a really decisive break with the two-dimensional past. At King's College, Cambridge and Fairford (Glos), for example, the effect is as if the glass-painters had punched holes in their picture plane to allow us to look beyond the immediate foreground into a middle distance and background teeming with activity. Over the shoulders of the figures we catch glimpses of convincing medieval townscapes and fertile countryside lit by sunlight (Plate 69).

71 *While the majority of animals in medieval glass are of the working variety, there are occasional glimpses of those creatures kept as pets and companions. One such is this little lap dog at the feet of Lady Margaret de Ros, depicted with great warmth and affection.*

(York Minster, N Yorks. St William Window. RCHME 1971)

8 Foreign Glass in England

So far, only glass made either by English medieval glaziers or glass commissioned by English medieval patrons from foreigners working for the most part in England itself has been considered. However, an important aspect of England's medieval stained glass heritage lies outside the realm of native works, for many of its churches contain important examples of foreign glass-painting of medieval date, collected from the early 19th century onwards and installed in English churches.

Although much new glass in a medieval style was commissioned in the course of the 19th century, numerous collectors purchased genuine medieval panels which then were installed in either medieval or Gothic Revival buildings. Circumstances in Europe in the late 18th and early 19th centuries were extremely favourable to these English collectors. The republican ideals of the French Revolution were accompanied by official atheism. In France itself, many churches were turned into temples of reason, while others, such as the Cathedral of Arras, were demolished. Many collectors shared the antiquarian Charles Winston's high regard for the intensely pictorial qualities of the early Renaissance and so panels such as those from the demolished church of St Jean in Rouen were highly sought after. Some of these can now be seen in York Minster. Three of the scenes are now in the Burrell collection in Glasgow, having once adorned Costessey Hall (Norfolk), and a further six scenes are in Wells Cathedral. In Oxfordshire the enterprising Rev J.B. Boteler acquired several fine panels of a Jesse Tree from the suppressed abbey church of St Bertin in St Omer, France, which were placed in Shiplake Parish Church (Oxon) in 1818. Two other fine Jesse Trees of similar date can be seen in St George's, Hanover Square, London and Wimborne Minster (Dorset). The former is from the church of St Jacques, Malines in Belgium.

In the early years of the 19th century, territorial ambition and revolutionary fervour carried republican ideals beyond the borders of France. Her victorious armies swept across Europe, and Belgium in particular suffered ecclesiastical despoilation as a result. The wealthy nunnery of Herckenrode was one such casualty. In 1797 its fittings, including its early 16th-century glass, were dispersed and the foundation closed. In 1802 most of the glass was purchased by Sir Brooke Boothby and subsequently given by him to Lichfield Cathedral (Staffs) where it was installed in the Lady Chapel by John Betton of Shrewsbury (Plate 72).

Another great Belgian loss of 1797 occurred when the Revolutionary Communal Council of Bruges sold the splendid windows from the royal Chapel of the Holy Rood for 14 francs a piece. They were subsequently bought

72   *This window depicting St Christopher and two kneeling donors contains 16th-century glass from the church of the Belgian nunnery of Herckenrode and was brought to England early in the 19th century. It has been installed in its new home with 19th-century embellishments, principally at its base.*

(Lichfield Cathedral, Staffs. RCHME 1982)

by an English collector and in 1918 were acquired by the Victoria & Albert Museum.

In 1794 French armies occupied the independent archdiocese of Cologne and sacked the Cathedral treasury. Quantities of glass from the Cologne area were displaced and found ready buyers in England (Plate 73a,b). The glass from the cloister of the Cistercian Abbey of Altenburg, suppressed in 1803, is one such example. One of its panels now resides in Marston Bigot Church (Somerset), while many more have found a home in the Victoria & Albert Museum. Eleven windows from the cloisters of the Premonstratensian Abbey of Steinfeld in the Eifel area of Germany were purchased by the Duke of Bridgewater. These windows were then installed in the chapel of Ashridge Park (Herts), built in the Gothic style by James Wyatt. Thirty-eight panels are now in the Victoria & Albert Museum, with eight panels at Erpingham in Norfolk, and more to be seen at Warham St Mary and Hevingham (both Norfolk).

One of the finest collections of foreign glass in any English church is in the parish church of St Mary, Shrewsbury (Shropshire). Pride of place goes to the nineteen panels depicting the Life of St Bernard of Clairvaux, also originally made for the cloisters of Altenburg. Also of German origin are several 15th-century panels from Trier of particular interest because of the votive inscriptions of the donors.

Belgian glass is also represented by two lights from the church of St Jacques in Liége and fragments from Herckenrode acquired by Rev W.G. Rowlands, Vicar of St Mary's from 1826 to 1828, who was also responsible for the acquisition of the Altenburg collection. The church also boasts a large collection of so-called 'Flemish' roundels, which were particularly popular among English collectors. These roundels were produced in large numbers in the 16th century in the ancient Low Countries. They were usually circular, approximately nine inches in diameter, although square and oval ones were made, and were executed on a single piece of white glass using only black or brown paint and yellow stain.

Apart from their obvious charm and the often exquisite quality of their workmanship, the interest of the roundels lies in their relationship to master-drawings and engravings of the period. As a result of religious unrest and war on the Continent, there are now relatively few surviving in their countries of origin, although many are to be found in England (Plate 74). A large number was donated by Mrs Colt of Rownhams House to the parish church of Rownhams in Hampshire, and a splendid collection (temporarily removed), including some later enamelled examples from Switzerland, can be seen in the parish church at Wragby (W Yorks). The use of roundels for decoration was not confined to churches, however. Several good examples are set into the doors and windows of Maristowe House, Bickleigh (Devon).

Alongside the partisans of early Renaissance glass-painting were those collectors who championed the merits of the early medieval styles, epitomized for many by the glass of Chartres. Thus Rivenhall (Essex) and Twycross (Leics) (Colour plate 14), are small parish churches containing fine French 12th-century glass from St Martin at Chenu and the royal abbey church of St Denis near Paris. In both cases these medieval panels have found new homes in medieval settings. The student of stained glass must therefore take care not to presume that medieval glass necessarily belongs in the medieval building in which it is found.

a

b

73 *Refined figures of the Virgin and Child with St Anne and kneeling donors, once in the possession of the Earls of Essex at Cassiobury Park (Herts). In style, they are related to glass surviving in the churches of Cologne, and this glass was probably displaced from its original home during the French invasion of the Archdiocese in 1794.*

(Church of St Mary, Stoke D'Abernon, Esher, Surrey. RCHME 1967).

74   *This roundel depicts an allegorical rather than a religious subject, showing the Triumph of Chastity, whose unicorn tramples the vanquished Cupid and Venus.*

(Church of St Helen, York, N Yorks. RCHME 1972)

One need not fear making such an error when in the church of St Mary and St Nicholas, Wilton (Wilts), where the medieval glass from a variety of sources, most notably St Denis, the Ste Chapelle and St Germain-des-Prés (Paris) and Rouen Cathedral nave has been installed in Thomas Henry Wyatt's extravagant version of Italian Romanesque, built 1841–5. The glass, which includes another panel from St Jacques in Malines, was given to the church in mid century by Sidney Herbert, Secretary of State for War, whose family home, Wilton House, is nearby.

Some impression of the quantity and variety of medieval glass imported into England in the 19th century can be gained by examining the account book of one of the period's most astute and successful dealers, John Christopher Hampp of Norwich. Hampp, a German by birth, was established by 1782 as a cloth merchant in Norwich. He imported glass mainly after the Peace of Amiens in 1802 and after the Battle of Leipzig in 1814.

His notebook, preserved in the Fitzwilliam Museum at Cambridge gives a tantalizing glimpse of the rich spoils of European war. Transactions with Rouen, Paris, Aachen, Cologne and Nuremburg all feature, but unfortunately, few of the panels described can now be identified with any certainty. The glass in Prittlewell Church (Essex) however, is known to have been acquired through Hampp and the glass from the Abbey of Steinfield (Germany) was almost certainly imported by him.

Although considerable work remains on the origins of much of the foreign glass in England, and particularly on the circumstances of its arrival here, it is an important and attractive addition to our native heritage.

Postscript

Thus far, only medieval stained glass has been examined, but no book on the subject would be complete without brief consideration of the 18th- and 19th-century background to the modern appreciation and preservation of medieval glass.

Something has already been said of the 19th-century craze for collecting medieval stained glass from all over Europe, by connoisseurs anxious to decorate their homes, private chapels and local parish churches and cathedrals. The collecting of foreign glass certainly did much to increase the esteem in which the native product was held. However, the revival of traditional glass-painting skills and medieval techniques also greatly helped to foster an atmosphere sympathetic to the preservation of medieval stained glass.

The roots of this new approach lay in the 18th century. In 1747 Horace Walpole purchased 'a little plaything house' close to the river at Twickenham and began to turn it into one of the most influential Gothic Revival buildings, Strawberry Hill. A rich collection of medieval stained glass was assembled and the enamel glass-painter, William Price the Younger (c.1703–65), was employed (1754 and 1759) to install it. Price had already encountered medieval glass at New College, Oxford and in creating a new set of windows for the south side of the chapel choir (c.1735–40) had incorporated 14th-century canopy work in his own compositions.

Upon Price's retirement, his younger contemporary, William Peckitt of York (1731–95), was called upon to work at Strawberry Hill and was also to contribute to the choir glazing of New College. Like Price before him, Peckitt was to preserve some of the medieval canopy and tracery work and in the canopies for his own figures there is an attempt to imitate, albeit loosely, the style of the late 14th-century canopy work. Peckitt's removal of the 14th-century west window, which led to its dispersal and partial destruction should be blamed as much on Peckitt's patrons as on the glass-painter himself.

Peckitt was to work as restorer at Exeter Cathedral (on the east window), but his most extensive restorations were to be in York Minster where, in addition to new windows (e.g. the south transept), he was entrusted with numerous medieval windows, most notably Archbishop Melton's west window. Peckitt's work for the west window (1757) has provoked much unjustified criticism. His most conspicuous additions were the heads of almost all the major figures, made necessary by the poor durability of the medieval glass used for much of the skin colour and possibly by earlier iconoclasm. He was working with the inferior glass of his day and the enamel colours at his disposal produced an effect quite unlike the work of his medieval predecessors, working in pot-metals. One is also reminded that Peckitt was not a good draughtsman (in his own work, he usually resorted to cartoons prepared by other artists). However, he was certainly not the heavy-handed philistine that his detractors so often maintain. In replacing the heads of the archbishops, Peckitt was able to preserve the surviving upper half of one 14th-century head, painting a lower half intended to imitate it in scale and style. That he appreciated the limitations of the materials available to him is suggested by the fact that he experimented in the production of more deeply coloured enamel stains and he claimed to have rediscovered the means of manufacturing pot-metal colours.

A far greater degree of skill and understanding of medieval style and technique was displayed in the restoration work of the Shrewsbury firm of Betton and Evans. John Betton (*c*.1765–1849) had been called upon to install the Herckenrode glass in Lichfield Cathedral (1806–8) and *c*.1815 took David Evans (1793–1861) into partnership. Probably their most important restoration work was undertaken between 1821 and 1828, when they were entrusted with the late 14th-century glass of Winchester College Chapel. They were asked 'to retouch the colours and restore the glass to its original condition'. This brief was disastrously interpreted as meaning the replacement of most of the original panels by accurate copies in garish colours quite unlike the sophisticated palette of the originals. However, a comparison of the copies with surviving originals demonstrates the degree to which David Evans had grasped the principles of the medieval craft.

Despite their valuable experience gained in the handling of medieval glass, neither Betton and Evans, nor their close contemporary, J.H. Miller (1777–1842), absorbed medieval principles into their own work, which remained essentially pictorial, attempting to achieve in stained glass the prevailing styles in oil painting. One of the first artists to absorb some of the lessons of the medieval craft into his own windows was Thomas Willement (1786–1871). In his work at Butleigh (Somerset) of 1829, the outlines of the design are carried in the leads in the medieval manner.

In all stained glass work of the early 19th century, the achievement of an authentic medieval effect (both in new windows and in the restoration of medieval windows) was limited by two factors: the quality of glass available and, perhaps more importantly, an imperfect understanding of historical styles.

The technical problem was solved mainly through the efforts of an amateur stained glass student, Charles Winston (1814–65). In 1849 he arranged the successful chemical analysis of medieval glass and persuaded the firm James Powell & Son of Whitefriars Glassworks in London to manufacture 'antique' glass. This was soon to be followed by a range of similar glass manufactured by W.E. Chance of Birmingham.

The 1840s were also to witness the publication of a number of influential works on historical styles. Antiquarian interest in medieval stained glass styles considerably pre-dates their appearance in new windows (Colour plate 15). Charles Winston was making accurate drawings of medieval glass of all periods as early as 1830. These academic enquiries were to reach a far wider audience with the appearance of *A Treatise on Painted Glass* by James Ballantine (1845), *An Inquiry into the Differences of Style Observable in Ancient Glass Paintings Especially in England: with Hints on Glass Painting* by Charles Winston (1847) and *A History of Stained Glass* by William Warrington (1848).

75 *The 14th-century windows of the Church of St John the Baptist, Hadzor were restored in 1866 by John Hardman & Co. The figure of the Virgin Annunciate is the most completely medieval, but this photograph demonstrates the skill and sensitivity with which the restoration was undertaken. The panels can now be seen in the Stained Glass Museum at Ely Cathedral.*

(Church of St John the Baptist, Hadzor, Hereford & Worcester. Gordon Barnes 1976)

Thus, the combination of technical advances and greater historical appreciation led to a more enlightened approach in the restoration of a number of important medieval windows in the 1850s and '60s. Winston himself was involved in work in Bristol Cathedral Lady Chapel (1847 and 1852–3), and Gloucester Cathedral east window (*c.*1860). Restoration work was also undertaken on the north rose window of Lincoln Cathedral (1855). All were to benefit from the better quality glass available and from the improved understanding of the intensions of the medieval originator.

If any one figure is to be regarded as the champion of the Gothic Revival both in architecture and in stained glass, that figure is A.W.N. Pugin, (1812–52) whose first executed church was begun in 1837. The Roman Catholic Pugin regarded Gothic as the only truly Christian style. For the execution of his stained glass designs, he was to employ two of Willement's pupils, William Warrington and Michael O'Connor, and from 1842 to 1845 was to turn to William Wailes of Newcastle. Pugin's force of conviction was influential on the work of the glass-painters who executed his designs. His most fruitful collaboration of all was with John Hardman of Birmingham, who began to manufacture stained glass in 1845 under Pugin's direct supervision. Their first triumph was the west window of Ushaw College, Durham (1847) and the Pugin-Hardman submissions for the Great Exhibition of 1851 were described as being in 'a class apart'. By the time of Pugin's death, in 1852, the triumph of Gothic over all other historical styles had largely been achieved and henceforth the care of the heritage of medieval stained glass was to rest (for the most part) in the hands of men whose technical skill approached and sometimes even surpassed that of the medieval masters (Plate 75).

Glossary of Terms

ABRADE To scrape or grind away a flashed surface (see below) to expose the base glass.

BACK PAINTING Painting applied to the exterior surface of the glass, usually confined to higher quality work.

BLACK LETTER The type of script used in stained glass from the 14th century onwards, in which black characters were painted on to white glass.

CALMES Grooved strips of lead, H-shaped in section, used to hold together the individual pieces of glass; found in various thicknesses.

CARTOON A full-size design for a window.

DIAPER A repeated motif, usually of a geometric design, used for background spaces.

FLASHING The application of a thin coat of coloured glass on a base glass, mostly white glass. Flashed ruby (red) is the most common.

GRISAILLE Geometric or leaf patterns painted on to white glass.

GROZING The method of shaping glass with a hooked metal tool, creating a characteristic 'nibbled' edge.

LOMBARDIC A form of script favoured in the 12th and 13th (and in some cases early 14th) centuries, in which capital letter forms were picked out of a layer of paint applied thickly to a base glass. This was a particularly legible script.

POT-METAL Glass coloured throughout by the addition of metal oxides when molten.

QUARRY A small pane of glass, usually diamond-shaped.

SMEAR SHADING An application of thin paint to the glass.

STICKWORK The removal of paint with a stick or brush-end before firing. Called 'scratching' when done with a needle point.

STIPPLING A method of shading by dabbing the paint surface.

YELLOW STAIN A stain ranging in colour from pale yellow to deep orange, produced by applying a solution of a silver compound to the glass, which turns yellow when fired. It is usually applied to the exterior surfaces.

Further Reading

Bibliography

Caviness, M.H. 1983 *Stained Glass before 1540*. G.K. Hall, Boston, distributed by MacMillan Publishers

General

Journals of the British Society of Master Glass-Painters 1924–present

Archer, D.M. 1985 *An Introduction to English Stained Glass*. HMSO
    A useful and up-to-date survey of English stained glass of all periods.
Baker, J. 1960 *English Stained Glass*. Thames & Hudson
    A short text but with marvellous illustrations.
Ballantine, J. 1845 *A Treatise on Painted Glass*. Chapman & Hall
    A work not entirely uncritical of the achievements of the medieval masters.
Coe, B. 1981 *Stained Glass in England: 1150–1550*. W.H. Allen
    An enjoyable introduction, arranged thematically.
Le Couteur, J.D. 1978 *English Medieval Painted Glass* (2nd edn). SPCK
    Although first published in 1926, and rather poorly illustrated, this remains one of the most erudite introductions to the subject.
Dodwell, C.R. 1961 *Theophilus: De Diversis Artibus*. Thomas Nelson & Sons
    A parallel Latin-English edition of the book on which our knowledge of medieval techniques rests.
Farmer, D.H. 1979 *The Oxford Dictionary of Saints*. OUP
    The most easily accessible book of its type.
James, M.R. 1924 *The Apocryphal New Testament*. OUP
    An invaluable English translation of all the apocryphal literature associated with the New Testament.
Moore, P. (ed) *Crown in Glory: A Celebration of Craftsmanship-Studies in Stained Glass*. Jarrold & Sons
    A collection of essays dedicated to conservator, Dennis King.
Rackham, B. 1936 *A Guide to the Collection of Stained Glass, Victoria & Albert Museum*. Victoria & Albert Museum
    An account of the best museum collection of stained glass in England.
Warrington, W. 1848 *The History of Stained Glass*. (Privately printed)
    The writer claimed to have restored medieval glass as early as 1833.

Westlake, N.H.J. 1881–94 *A History in the Design of Painted Glass.* (4 vols) James Parker
    One of the earliest and most meticulous considerations of evolving styles in medieval stained glass.

Winston, C. 1847 *An Inquiry into the Differences of Style Observable in Ancient Glass Paintings Especially in England with Hints on Glass Painting.* J. H. Parker
    The first serious attempt to subject medieval stained glass to art-historical scrutiny.

    1865 *Memoirs Illustrative of the Art of Glass Painting.* J.H. Parker
    Contains valuable accounts of Winston's involvement in early conservation.

Woodforde, C. 1954 *English Stained and Painted Glass.* OUP
    Another general survey of glass of all periods. Interesting illustrations.

Monuments and Places

Caviness, M.H. 1981 *The Windows of Christ Church Cathedral, Canterbury.* Corpus Vitrearum Medii Aevi Great Britain. Vol II. British Academy

Colchester, L.S. 1977 *The Stained Glass in Wells Cathedral* (5th edn). Friends of Wells Cathedral

Drake, F.M. 1913 The painted glass of Exeter Cathedral and other Devon churches. *Archaeological Journal* Vol LXX

French, T.W. and O'Connor, D.E. 1987 *The West Windows of the Nave.* Corpus Vitrearum Medii Aevi Great Britain. Vol III, 1. British Academy

Ganderton, E.W. and Lafond, J. 1961 *Ludlow Stained and Painted Glass.* Friends of St Lawrence Church

Green, M.A. Old painted glass in Worcestershire. *Worcestershire Archaeological Society* (New series) Vols XI-XXIX

Harvey, J.H. and King, G. 1971 Winchester College stained glass. *Archaeologia* Vol CIII

Haselock, J. and O'Connor, D.E. 1980 The medieval stained glass of Durham Cathedral. *Medieval Art and Architecture at Durham Cathedral* (British Archaeological Association Transactions for the Year 1977) Vol III

Hutchinson, F.E. 1949 *Medieval Glass at All Souls College.* Faber & Faber

Kerr, J. 1985 The east window at Gloucester Cathedral. *Medieval Art and Architecture at Gloucester and Tewkesbury* (British Archaeological Association Transactions for the Year 1981) Vol VII

Knowles, J.A. 1936 *Essays in the History of the York School of Glass Painting.* OUP

Le Couteur, J.D. 1920 *Ancient Glass in Winchester.* Warren & Son

Marks, R. 1982 The medieval stained glass of Wells Cathedral. Colchester, L.S. (ed) *Wells Cathedral, a History.* Open Books

Morgan, N.J. 1983 *The Medieval Painted Glass of Lincoln Cathedral.* Corpus Vitrearum Medii Aevi Great Britain. Occasional Papers 3. British Academy

Newton, P.A. 1979 *The County of Oxford. A Catalogue of Medieval Stained Glass.* Corpus Vitrearum Medii Aevi Great Britain. Vol I. British Academy

O'Connor, D.E. and Haselock, J. 1977 The stained and painted glass. Aylmer, G.E. and Cant, R. (eds) *A History of York Minster*. OUP

Peatling, A.V. 1930 Ancient stained and painted glass in the churches of Surrey. *Transactions of the Surrey Archaeological Society*

Pitcher, S.A. 1925 Ancient stained glass in Gloucestershire churches. *Transactions of the Bristol and Gloucestershire Archaeological Society* Vol XLVII

Rackham, B. 1949 *The Ancient Glass of Canterbury Cathedral*. Lund Humphries

Rushforth, G.M. 1922 The great east window of Gloucester Cathedral. *Transactions of the Bristol and Gloucestershire Archaeological Society* Vol XLIV

1924 The glass in the quire clerestory of Tewkesbury Abbey. *Transactions of the Bristol and Gloucestershire Archaeological Society* Vol XLVI

1936 *Medieval Christian Imagery: Great Malvern Priory Church*. OUP

Smith, M.Q. 1983 *The Stained Glass of Bristol Cathedral*. Friends of Bristol Cathedral. Redcliffe Press

Toy, J. 1985 *A Guide and Index to the Windows of York Minster*. Dean and Chapter of York

Wayment, H. 1972 *The Windows of King's College Chapel, Cambridge*. Corpus Vitrearum Medii Aevi Supplementary Vol 1. British Academy

1984 *The Stained Glass of the Church of St Mary, Fairford, Gloucestershire*. Society of Antiquaries

Welander, D. 1985 *The Stained Glass of Gloucester Cathedral*. Dowland Press

Woodforde, C. 1946 *Stained Glass in Somerset 1250–1830*. OUP

1950 *The Norwich School of Glass Painting in the 15th Century*. OUP

1951 *The Stained Glass of New College, Oxford*. OUP

Index

Parish churches are listed under place name. References to plate numbers are in bold type.